OLD WEST COOKBOOK

Copyright © 1987
First Published in 1987 by Evans Publications, Perkins, Oklahoma 74059
All rights reserved. No part of this book may be reproduced except for short excerpts
for book review purposes.
Printed in the United States of America
Library of Congress Catalog Card Number: 86-81884
ISBN 0-934188-23-8

BARBARA BLACKBURN'S OLD WEST COOKBOOK

Contents

TX
715
.B557
1987

Foreword vii
Introduction ix
Acknowledgements xi

CHAPTERS
1. The Spirit of the West 1
   Beverages 3
2. Grains of Truth 11
   Batters and Doughs 13
3. Vanishing Vittles 31
   Puddings and Porridges 32
4. Cast Iron Cookery 38
   Soups and Stews 39
5. The Call of the Wild 54
   Surf and Turf, Meat, Poultry and Fish 55
6. Eating What Comes Naturally 71
   Vegetables 73
7. Milk Buckets, Butter Churns, and Egg Baskets 85
   Egg and Dairy Products 86
8. Preserving the Past 92
   Relishes and Preserves 93
9. Sweet Somethings 104
   Desserts 105
10. Household Hints 130

   Bibliography 142
   Index 143

Dedicated To Jim Dullenty

He helped me blaze the trail of Old West cooking by giving me my Old West Cookery column, through which I met the fine people who provided me with many of my recipes. . .

BARBARA BLACKBURN'S OLD WEST COOKBOOK

There probably is no one in America better able to produce a cookbook on Old West cooking than Barbara Blackburn, author of this book. That's because for the past several years Barbara has been in the unique position of having hundreds of Old West recipes sent to her in her capacity as Old West Recipe editor for Western Publications (*True West, Frontier Times and Old West* magazines).

Barbara's interest in natural and frontier cooking goes back many years and since 1982 her Old West cookery stories have regularly appeared in Western Publications' magazines. She also has had recent appearances in *Real West, American West* and *Roundup*, the magazine of the Western Writers of America. In fact, it is getting so if you pick up a western magazine, you are likely to find Barbara Blackburn within its covers. Through hard work and tenacity she is making herself preeminent in the world of western cookery and this cookbook will help assure that position.

Barbara does something that all cookery columnists should do, even when she publishes other people's recipes, as she does in Old West recipe column: she tests each and every recipe. She cooks the dish and serves it, for reaction, to a stalwart husband and two inquisitive children. Her husband, a meteorologist, and children are severe critics of the food they receive so if it passes their taste test, then she knows it has to be good.

Barbara was already deeply involved in cookery writing when she came to my attention in 1982. At the time I was editor of Western Publications' magazines, and she submitted a story on the use of herbs in pioneer cooking.

The magazines in 1979 had been purchased from their longtime owner, Joe "Hosstail" Small by Chet Krause of Krause Publications, Iola, Wisconsin. By 1982, when I became editor, Chet had acquired a controlling interest and was determined to expand the features in the magazines. One of many ways this was done was to offer an Old West cookery column.

Old West cooking was added because we discovered from a survey made in 1981, that more than 75 percent of the readership of the magazines were men. To expand our appeal, we added the cooking column to attract women. But the column became as popular with men as women judging from the recipes sent in by readers.

When Barbara's story on herbal cooking landed on my desk it came at an opportune time. I was casting about for ways to find western cooking writers and here was one knocking at the door. Barbara's story had more to do with pioneering in general, than in the West, so I returned it to her for some revisions. And, as she does with everything, she quickly revised the story to make it acceptable and it appeared in Winter 1982 *Old West* as "Herbs and Other Greens are Back in Flavor."

That began Barbara's association with Western Publications which continues to this day.

Not content to sit back at home and receive the recipes sent in, Barbara goes into the field, a sort of Julia Child of the West. She has traveled extensively all over much of the West—she has plans for another trip this summer—and in her travels she has discovered regional cookbooks, old recipes and other aids to her writing.

So whether Barbara Blackburn is writing about buffalo steaks or sipping sarsparilla (she spent weeks researching this old western drink, finally sending the editor a story along with a good supply of sarsparilla bark), you know when you enjoy her writing and prepare dishes based on her recipes, that everything is authentic. She'll not only tell you how to make it like Grandma used to, but she'll tell you what modern substitutes can be made in case certain items are not available.

Who will ever forget Barbara's recipe for Beehive Apple Pie, in a recent *Frontier Times*? Came right out of the cooking experiences of the Mormons who moved west in handcarts. That's what Old West cooking is all about.

—Jim Dullenty
Hamilton, Montana

INTRODUCTION

The palate like the heart does not change and we can "go home again" with some of these fine old foods in this book. It is the hope that this will be more than just a cookbook, but a history of the frontier and other areas of the United States from 1840 to 1910. The recipes in the "West" came from New England, the Middle Atlantic and even the South and Southwest. When the pioneers took their utensils and recipes west with them, they often adapted these recipes to the new foods they found along the way and the new areas in which they settled. Some of the same ingredients even without new partners found new names but were basically the same old dishes.

The recipes that appear simple to us were not so simple for the frontierswomen in the 19th century. What took almost a whole day to prepare can be put together in no time with modern equipment. The fact that many of these old foods face extinction, even though they are often "just plain food" gives them a rare quality, that could lend the name gourmet. Today an honest dish of mashed potatoes is not as easy to come by as a one of "chemicalized" rice pilaf—and you know what I'm talking about if you eat in restaurants at all. If you want to eat honest food these days with ingredients normally stocked in the kitchen, you have to do what great-grandma did—cook it yourself.

My own interest in food and preparation has encompassed just about every cuisine on earth, having traveled and sampled many foods of other lands and of other times. I like to use a lot of herbs gathered (and dried when in surplus) from my own garden. If I am out of an ingredient and it is not time for the weekly shopping trip, I like to play what I call "Mother Hubbard's Cupboard," that is making do with what you have. This has created my most delightful recipes; as they say "Necessity is the mother of invention." The pioneer lady did the very same thing; it was much more mandatory. In these modern days it is no longer necessary to shoot a blackbird for your dinner. However, you might take a lesson from the past and forage for some spring greens, like nutritious dandelions.

Our ancestors were not too concerened about excess fat, salt, and sugar. Cholesterol was not a household word, but lard was. Personally, I like the flavor and texture that the "rendered fat" added to some of the old foods, and it tastes better than the "hygrogenated fluff." Maybe with a little more exercise and some excess fiber from the whole grains we won't have to be too concerned about the foods with the high calorie count. Salt, on the other hand, is something of not much value to me. Most recipes, except for baked goods where salt affects the rising action, list salt as optional. Personally, I think it spoils the real taste, and if you want variety in flavor, herbs and spices do it much better.

This book is the result of several years of intense study and testing (using my favorite technique, "taste as you go") of many recipes mostly sent to me from people all over the country west of the Mississippi, although I have to admit that my kitchen is located east of the Mississippi. But as one of my Western writer

friends, Chuck Parsons, said to me, "The West is a state of mind." And these recipes will taste just as good and be just as authentic no matter where your kitchen is. What matters is that you want to preserve the flavors of the past.
—Barbara Blackburn

Corn bread was often the staff of life for the pioneers of the past.

Acknowledgements

As time moves on original sources become fewer. Luckily, we were able to collect recipes from some old-timers who knew the Old West. If they did not experience directly, our other contributors were party to tales from their families, and are guardians of cherished scrapbooks and collections of "culinary antiques." With a special thanks as vast as those wide open spaces I wish to thank all of the readers who sent in recipes, originally to qualify for the recipe of the month, and then for the first published collection of *True West* recipes. A few of the recipes have already appeared in the pages of the magazines. I wish to give credit to a few who supplied me with a collection of tasty tidbits, some collected for their own writings:

Bill Austin, Julie Anton, Mabel Bays, Dorothy Breeding—my mother, Louise Blackburn—my mother-in-law, Davilla Bright—I learned a lot about homesteading in "The Sooner State" from her, Paul and Olive Brunner, M. Butchee, Mrs. Lester Christian, T. D. Church, Margaret Daniels, La Nelle E. Davis, William Dunn, James Furry, Don Getz—whose contributions are as spirited as his sourdough starter, Helen Grainger, Hollis W. Harris, Kenneth Heffling, Bobbye and Bernice Herzberg, Russel E. Hill, Alice Jacobs, Tom R. Kovach, Bill Lantz, Mrs. Neil Leist, George McCrary, Judy Michaels—whose household hints were very valuable, Mary Anne McDonald, John W. Moore, Hattie Nevin, John Norwood—known for his railroad stories and others in the magazines, William Newton, Waldo Olson, Bill O'Neal—a "Real" help with newspaper clippings of old recipes, Jean and Rich Peterson, Katherine Place, Ellen E. Pope, LaVerne E. Ray, B. H. Roach, Eloise Rushing, Edith Schiller, Ardis Shilton, Edith Scholey, Carolyn Stewart, Mrs. Don Swank, Bonnie Swayze, Lenora Taylor, Joe Teague, Mrs. Carl Teasley, Walt Thayer—an old cartoonist with a sense of humor and lots of postage, Winnie Thorne, Bertha Trelling, Vivian Turnbull, and Naomi Wood.

Thanks to the Buffalo and Erie County Public Library for lots of good secondary sources.

I especially want to thank my favorite test panel participant—my husband Alan. He's really a Westerner and an adventuresome eater. Thanks to my mother, too, who sampled and enjoyed many of the foods, and let all her friends know what a fine cookbook this is . . . . And to my children, Trina and Brad, growing up in a world of "golden arches". . .well, thanks for joining us for those unique dinners!

A special thanks to my partner in publishing, John Joerschke, present editor of *True West* magazine; he edited the original manuscript for the book. But the biggest thanks of all goes to Jim Dullenty, former editor of the magazine, who made Old West Cookery a permanent part of our lives.

THE SPIRIT OF
THE WEST

A fiddle, a rifle, an axe, and a Bible sometimes were not enough for characters who settled the West. Trappers and traders, prospectors and pioneers, outlaws and lawmen, cowboys and Indians often turned to bottled cheer. Westerners were ingenious in transforming anything natural—grains, berries, and even bark—into intoxicating beverages.

The Southwest's best-known intoxicant was Tiswin, a fermented drink made by the Apaches. Women and children soaked corn overnight. Then they dug a long trench and covered it with a layer of grass. After being sprinkled with water morning and evening for ten days, the corn in the trench sprouted. The sprouted corn was ground and boiled for four or five hours. The liquid was strained off and set aside. After about 24 hours it stopped bubbling and was ready to drink. Tiswin's alcoholic content was low, but the Apaches often drank so much of it they became quite intoxicated.

Frontier winemakers did not rely solely on grapes. Just about any growing plant would do. Homemade parsnip wine, similar to sherry, was popular, especially among circuit-riding clergymen and old maids. Apples made wine or fermented cider, one of the most popular. There was a wine for every season. Dandelions were gathered for wine in the spring. In the summer, rose petals were used. Celery wine was a fall favorite. What kind of wine could be made in the winter? On the cold and grim frontier that was the season when more wine was consumed than made.

Great-grandmother's herb garden boosted wine-making. Clary wine was brewed from sage. Secret touches such as dropping a handful of clary sage blossoms into the cask after the fermenting had started were added. Comfrey made a nutritious wine, as did coltsfoot. They were used not only to boost spirits but also to "cure" physical ailments. Herbal wines were used to prevent diseases—big reason indeed for a little indulgence!

The list of berries used in wine seems endless: mulberries, rowanberries, whortleberries, bilberries, blackberries, chokecherries, huckleberries, and serviceberries. Gooseberries made the champagne of the Old West. Elderberries made a rich, dry wine which, beside flavoring Christmas puddings, fruitcakes, and casseroles, remedied colds. For her nightcap, Granny sipped elderberry wine laced with cayenne pepper.

Some strange ingredients also went into beer in the good ol' days. Nettle beer purified blood and it still had a "sting." Treacle beer was flavored with molasses. Many recipes for homemade beer in the last century called for such woodsy products as sassafras and spruce. Though most beers today are pasteurized and taste considerably different than those, ginger beer is still available in a few stores.

Rye whiskey was the drink of choice saloons; red likker was in the far west establishments. Other names for similar hard stuff were skullbender, tongue oil,

Sarsaparilla and Switchel were popular thirst quenchers.

corpse reviver, snakehead whiskey, tangleleg, and tarantula juice. Tangleleg was a blend of tobacco, molasses, red peppers, and raw alcohol.

Whiskey wasn't always the spirit. Torchlight whiskey was really cheap gin. The Swedes of North Dakota concocted "wedding whiskey" from grain alcohol, burned sugar, and crushed peaches. Herbs were added to this aphrodisiac blend "to make the bridegroom go." A favorite drink in Montana was Shelby Lemonade, a mix of alkai water, alcohol, tobacco juice and a dash of strychnine to keep the heart going.

The plusher establishments served high quality drinks. Hotel bars in Denver and Colorado Springs, Colorado, specialized in a giant glass filled half with porter and half with champagne. A "mule skinner" was whiskey with blackberry liquor. Bob Stockton's saloon in Denver was the only place outside of New Orleans to obtain Sazerac.

The saloon didn't have a corner on spirits. The medicine man sold Hotstetter's Bitters, a "liver-regulator" and cure for chilblains, dyspepsia, evil humor, loose bowels, torpidness and ague. This panacea was the lowest grade double-distilled whiskey with just a touch of honey. Clergymen favored it and visited the pharmacist without guilt.

Then there was B. J. Kendall's blackberry balsam remedy for diarrhea, dysentery, cholera, biliousness, and liver problems. Each fluid ounce of this sixty-one percent alcohol solution contained five grains of opium. With its similarly high alcoholic content, Dr. Simmon's Regulator for Liver was labeled a "cowboy's friend." Dr. Sweet's Infallible Liniment promised to raise hair on a bald man's head and strengthen the roots if taken internally. Leading the elixirs, though, was Limerick's Great Southern Liniment, warranted to cure twenty-seven disorders!

Not even prohibition could extinguish the spirit of the West. Lemon extract, a refresher reverenced by Texans, came to the rescue. They would chip a hole in a cake of ice and fill it up with extract. The syrup became gooey and hardened; then the remaining alcohol could be poured off and made into drinks.

CHAPTER 1
Beverages
With and Without the Spirit

COWBOY COFFEE

Coffee beans, freshly ground.

What makes cowboy coffee **cowboy** coffee? You dump the grounds right into the water! An old cowboy made his coffee by filling an old enamel pot with water and pouring in about half a cup of ground coffee. He cooked it over an open fire or wood stove until it boiled over.

Use any pan, kettle or pot you have. Put as many cups of water into the pot as you want and turn on the heat. When the water boils, remove the pot and wait until water stops boiling. Then stir in about one rounded tablespoon of regular grind coffee per cup of water. Let stand a couple of moments until the grounds settle; then pour gently.

Real cowboys couldn't care less about a few grounds in their teeth, and they liked their coffee strong. Some tested it by seeing if it would float a silver dollar; others used a horseshoe.

Put as many cups of water into the pot as you want and turn on the heat. When the water boils remove the pot. Then stir in about one rounded tablespoon of regular grind coffee per cup of water. Let the grounds settle. Toss a shoe from a club-footed horse into the pot. Gaze steadily into the pot. If the hoss-shoe ain't floatin', your coffee ain't ready.

This wisdom came from S. Omar Baker, well-known Western poet and humorist. If you don't mind a few grounds, the coffee (without the shoe) will taste great.

IMITATION COFFEE

The pioneers often had no real coffee, but being the resourceful folks they were, concocted a substitute. If you can't tell the difference, you've been smoking too many hand-rolled cigarettes...

6 c. bran
3 c. cornmeal
1 c. molasses
1 tsp. salt
2 eggs

Brown in oven after mixing together. Let dry. Use as coffee.

Jean and Rich Peterson of Correctionville, Iowa sent this recipe. They are kin to some notorious outlaws and lawmen. Through Jean's grandfather's mother's side, Jean is related to Belle Starr. Imagine Belle having a cup of this imitation coffee.

Cornmeal, bran, molasses, eggs and salt make Frontier Coffee.

HARD TIMES COFFEE

Bernice Herzberg, of Elsberry, Missouri, submitted a slightly different recipe for imitation coffee:

2 qts. wheat bran
1 pt. yellow cornmeal
3 well-beaten eggs
1 c. best sorghum molasses

Mix bran and cornmeal. Add eggs and molasses. Beat well; spread on pan and put to dry in oven. Use great care by stirring often while it is browning. This is the secret of good coffee. A handful is sufficient for two persons. Sweet cream improves the flavor of the brew, but as with store-bought coffee, this is a matter of personal taste.

MILK COFFEE

Boil milk or cream separately, and bring to table in covered vessel. Pour into coffee.

CAMPFIRE COFFEE

1 qt. cold water plus
½ c. cold water
1 c. ground coffee
1 egg

Heat a quart of water to boiling. Boil 2 to 3 minutes. Add one cup of coffee grounds per quart of water to boiling water. Mix in an egg, shell and all. Boil 4 minutes more. Then add ½ cup cold water to settle the grounds. When the grounds and eggshell, which acts as a binder, have settled, the coffee is superb.

Arbuckles coffee won the West. At one time, to each brown paper bag of Arbuckles coffee a stick of peppermint candy was attached as a premium. The package labels could be redeemed for prizes such as razors and clocks.

HERB TEA

You can make tea with any herb you please. Use a heaping tablespoon of the fresh herb or one teaspoon of the dried herb, plus one measure for the pot. Pour boiling water over the herbs and steep gently about five minutes, more or less, depending on how strong you want it.

The herb tea can be iced. Try a combination of mints and chamomille for this simple mint tea:

Place about eight large stalks of fresh mint in a saucepan and pour about six cups of water over them. Bring slowly to a boil and remove from heat. Cover and steep 5-8 minutes until tea is the right strength.

CHOCOLATE

To each square of chocolate allow 3 jills or a chocolate cup and a half of boiling water. Scrape down chocolate with a knife. Mix into paste with just enough hot water to melt the chocolate. Add to the rest of the water; set over hot coals and cover. Boil (stirring twice) till liquid is reduced by one-third. Supply with cream or rich milk and serve immediately. If you want it frothed, twirl in it the little wooden instrument called a chocolate mill.

Now isn't that a lot more interesting than today's hot chocolate?

SOUTHWESTERN MOCHA

4 oz. or 4 squares Mexican chocolate or sweet cooking chocolate
4 c. rich milk
½ tsp. or more ground cinnamon
2 eggs
½ tsp. finely grated orange peel
½ tsp. vanilla extract
½ c. dark roast black coffee

Melt chocolate in double boiler; whisk in milk and cinnamon. Heat for 15 minutes. Whisk eggs with peel and vanilla and stream in the hot chocolate, whisking constantly. Add coffee and beat to a froth. Serve at once with a stick of cinnamon, optional.

With the Spirit . . .

GINGER BEER

This spirited beverage was a frontier favorite. Judith F. Michaels, of Yucaipa, California, sent the recipe from a 1902 HOW TO DO book. The more modest version will yield plenty of this powerful brew.

11 oz. bruised ginger root
9 gal. water
½ lb. honey
3 pts. yeast
10 lbs. sugar
9 oz. lemon juice or 1 cup and 2 T.
½ oz. essence of lemon
1 white of an egg

Boil the ginger root half an hour in a gallon of water; then add the rest of the water and the other ingredients. Strain when cold. Add the white of an egg beaten and the essence of lemon; let stand four days. Then bottle. It will keep many months.

MORE MODEST VERSION

3 oz. bruised ginger root
3 gal. water
⅓ lb. honey
2 oz. yeast
2 lb. sugar
4 oz. lemon juice
½ tsp. lemon extract
white of an egg

Follow above directions.

MOLASSES BEER

6 qt. water
2 qt. West Indian molasses
½ pt. brewer's yeast
1 T. ground ginger
1 T. cream of tartar
raisins

Stir ingredients together, except raisins. Let stand 12 hours, then bottle, putting 3 or 4 raisins in each bottle. The raisins stop the fermentation. This beer keeps 2 to 3 days in a cool place, longer in today's refrigerator.

GINGER BEER

Soft drinks a century ago were not so "soft," having an alcoholic content. Ginger beer was often a tonic. Ginger ale today is prescribed for stomach upsets, but the ginger drink of yesteryear was more natural and more powerful:

1½ lbs. loaf sugar
3 oz. strong white ginger
grated peel of 2
  lemons and the juice

2½ gal. boiling water
2 large T. of strong yeast

Combine sugar, ginger and peel. Put into a large stone jar; pour over the boiling water. When tepid, strain and add juice of lemons and the yeast. Let stand overnight, then "bottle" in ½ pint stone bottles, "tying down the cork with twine."

SASSAFRAS BEER

2 gal. soft water
1 qt. sheaf bran
1 handful dried apples
½ pt. molasses
1 small handful of hops

piece of sassafras root
  size of egg
½ pint of strong fresh yeast
2 large T. ginger, optional

Put all ingredients except molasses and yeast in large kettle. Boil till apples are soft. Strain molasses into liquor and when lukewarm, stir in yeast. Put into kegs or jugs and let stand uncorked to ferment. Fill jugs full to enable the fermenting liquor to run over. Set in a large tub. When fermenting has subsided, cork. It can be drunk the next day. Added ginger is an improvement. You can tell it is ready when it is bubbling as much as carbonated soda.

Some pretty strange things went into beer in those early days.

SPRUCE BEER

10 gal. water
1 lb. hops
1 c. ginger
6 qts. molasses

3½ oz. essence of
  spruce
½ pt. yeast

Combine water, hops, and ginger. Boil together until the hops sink to the bottom. Dip out a bucket of the liquor and stir in the molasses and spruce. (You can substitute two pounds of outer sprigs of spruce.) When dissolved, pour liquor into kettle. Strain through a sieve into a cask; stir in the yeast. Let it ferment a day or two; then bottle it the next day. To prevent further fermentation, put three or four raisins in each bottle.

BEE BEER

Yes, back in the Old West beers were made of all natural ingredients. Soda pop developed from what were called small beers, having up to ten percent alcohol. Strong, dark honey was used to make mead or bee beer, on ranches in California and other areas in the West.

Set one part honey to three parts warm rain water and stir until the honey is melted. Float toast on the top and cover with a clean cloth until it works. To help introduce the yeast, use one teaspoon of dry active yeast to each gallon of water. When the beer begins the fermentation process and creates a frothy head it is working.

When "done," cork down and put in the cellar until needed. It will be done, or ready to bottle, when it is bubbling about as much as carbonated, sparkling soda. It will take from three to ten days depending on the weather.

Use clean bottles that take crown caps and can withstand pressure. Champagne bottles work best. Lay the capped bottles on their sides in a relatively cool place for at least 3 months.

To drink, chill each bottle thoroughly before uncapping. Decant into other containers. This should be an effervescent golden brew with an alcoholic content about that of most ales.

Wines and Cordials

These drinks were good tonics for both prevention and cure, but a pound of prevention was always better than an ounce of cure. . .

GOOSEBERRY WINE

3 gal. boiled soft water
6 gal. full ripe gooseberries
loaf sugar
brandy and eggs, optional

In a wooden dish crush and mash berries, a few at a time. Pour boiling water on mashed berries; cover, and let stand 12 hours. Strain and measure juice; to each quart allow ¾ pounds loaf sugar. Mix and let stand 8 or 9 hours to dissolve. Reserve some liquor. Pour the rest into a keg; let ferment at the bung holes, filling the keg to the top to replace the liquor that works out. As soon as it ceases to hiss, close with cloth wrapped around the bung.

A pint of white brandy for every gallon of gooseberry wine may be added on bunging it up. It's best bottled in cold, frosty weather. Refine further by allowing to every gallon of wine the whites of 2 eggs beaten to a froth. Mix well with a quart of wine; pour into a cask, and in a few days it will be fine and clear.

Brandy is double distilled wine. White brandy is usually the raw product that has not been aged in wood. Aging in the oak casks gives brandy its color, unless caramel coloring is added. This clear white liquid is also known as eau de vie, or water of life.

CURRANT WINE

4 gal. ripe currants, mashed
2½ gal. water
5 lbs. loaf sugar

Optional:
2 beaten egg whites
½ oz. cream of tartar
brandy

Let currants stand two hours; put into a linen bag and squeeze into a jar. Boil together the water and sugar, skimming well. Mix with juice. Let stand 2-3 weeks to settle; then transfer to another vessel, not disturbing the dregs. If not clear, refine by mixing the egg whites with the cream of tartar with some of the wine, then with all the wine. Let stand 10 days and bottle. Place bottles on sides in sawdust (not from pine wood). This is fit to drink in a year, but it is better in 3-4 years. When working the wine, a little brandy can be added to fortify it, about one quart of brandy.

ELDERBERRY WINE

Do you remember your grandma's elderberry wine? How about your great-grandma's? Try this when you are not feeling so well . . . or when you are.

12 qts. boiling water
4 qts. stemmed elderberries
6¾ c. sugar

3 tsp. ground ginger
8 whole cloves
1 lb. seeded raisins
brandy, optional

Pour boiling water on berries, and let stand for 24 hours. Strain through coarse bag or cloth, squeezing and breaking berries to extract all possible juice. Bring to boil and simmer for 1 hour, skimming frequently. Cool to lukewarm. Measure and, if brandy is used, add ½ cup to each 4 quarts of mixture. Let stand for 2 weeks to ferment. Then put in bottles and keep several months in a cool place before using. Makes 8 quarts.

Cordials were more than after dinner drinks; they were fine medicines and simple pleasures any time of day or night.

RASPBERRY CORDIAL

Squeeze ripe berries through a linen bag. To each quart juice allow 1 pint white brandy and ½ pound powdered loaf sugar. Let stand 2 weeks in glass jar. Filter and bottle. The same can be done with strawberries.

QUINCE CORDIAL

Grate the pulp and let stand in tureen 24 hours. Squeeze through jelly bag. To 6 quarts juice allow 1 pint cold water, 3 pounds broken up loaf sugar, and 1 quart of white brandy. Mix and put in a stone jar. Have 3 flannel bags, not larger than a 2-inch square, 1 filled with nutmeg, 1 with powdered mace, and 1 with powdered cloves. Add to the liquid. Leave jar uncorked a few days, reserving some of the liquid to replace that lost in fermentation. When done working, bottle. Don't use for 6 months. Filter through fine muslin if the cordial is not clear.

ROSE CORDIAL

Break fresh rose leaves into a tureen with a quart of lukewarm water. Let infuse for 24 hours. Squeeze through linen bag until the liquid is pressed out. Put a fresh pound of rose leaves into tureen; pour liquid back, and let infuse again for 2 days. Repeat until strong. Then to a pint of infusion add ½ pound of loaf sugar, ½ pint white brandy, 1 ounce broken cinnamon, 1 ounce coriander seeds. Put into glass jar and let stand 2 weeks. Filter through fine muslin or white blotting paper pinned on the bottom of a sieve.

Holiday Beverage Recipes

HOT SPICED APPLEJACK

A fiddle, and a guitar were often not enough for the pioneers. Along with these they needed a little bottled cheer like this recipe for hot spiced applejack, given to me by my mother-in-law, Louise Hill Blackburn.

4 c. applejack or
   cider and applejack mixed
maple syrup to taste

1 tsp. grated cloves
1 tsp. allspice

Heat ingredients and serve warm.

MULLED CIDER

To a quart of cider add a handful of whole cloves and boil. Beat 6 eggs in large pitcher, adding sugar. Pour boiling cider on the beaten eggs and pour back and forth from one pitcher to another till you have a fine froth. Pour warm into glasses and grate nutmeg over.

MULLED WINE

In 1 pint wine put 2 unbeaten nutmegs, a handful of broken cinnamon, and a handful of slightly pounded cloves. Heat to boiling. When liquid is reduced to ½, strain in a quart of port wine. Heat again. Serve hot, with a plate of rusk.

BISHOP

Roast 4 large whole oranges until a light brown. Dissolve ½ pound sugar and 1 T. cinnamon into ½ pint claret. Quarter oranges. Lay in bottom of bowl and add 2 beaten or grated nutmegs and some more cinnamon. Pour the wine and sugar over the oranges. Cover and let stand until the next day. Heat the rest of claret to almost boiling. Mash pieces of oranges and bring out the juice. Skim into the hot claret. Serve warm.

SANGAREE

Combine ⅓ part wine, ale or porter, with ⅔ warm or cold water. Add sugar to sweeten and then grate nutmeg over this. To make NEGUS, add lemon juice.

GRAINS OF TRUTH

The harvest from the tilled fields on the frontier was the basis for bread and other whole-grain goodies. Bread was indeed the staff of life. There were many alternatives to bread in pioneer homes: dumplings, cornbread, griddle cakes, bannocks, muffins, and biscuits. All of those had as many variations as bread had yeast cells.

The pioneer bread was not supposed to be light. Neither the flour was bleached nor the germ removed. At the turn of the century bakers' bread became a status symbol, when people could afford it. Cowboys called such bread "gun waddin" or wasp's nest.

Early bread started with cornmeal but also could include rye, wheat, or acorn flour. Buckwheat was popular for pancakes. Salt-rising bread was used in many pioneer households. It started with a natural ferment but could not be expanded by doubling as sourdough. Salt-rising was also a good bread to make while enroute to breaking new ground.

The most famous bread of the Old West was sourdough. To the goldseekers who went West the sourdough starter was a treasure in itself. If a man had his crock of sourdough and a sack of flour, he was at least assured of something to eat. Often the sourdough starter was the last thing to be placed in the sack and the first to be removed upon reaching the destination. When it was cold at night the "old sourdough" cuddled up to his starter under the blankets. And if it were cold during the day, that oldtimer even wore the starter, in some material, around his neck. If the sourdough starter turned green, it was to be discarded.

For the pioneer housewife, sourdough was a staple. She sometimes shared a part of her starter with a new pioneer family, as a welcoming gesture of friendship. The sourdough was used in other products besides bread, such as pancakes, biscuits, and muffins.

The chuck wagon cook savored his sourdough to make his famous flapjacks and biscuits over the campfire. His Dutch oven and his skillet did wonders with the sourdough. The cook often kept the starter inside the flour barrel, stored in the chuck wagon.

Both the chuck wagon cook and the pioneer woman made quick breads. Although the person who named these popular members of the bread family remains a mystery, why they are so named is obvious. They are easier to make and take less time than the ones made with yeast. Quick breads are leavened by baking powder or baking soda and sometimes by steam. They can be grouped according to the thickness or thinness of the batter. There are pour batters and drop batters and soft doughs which are to be rolled, patted out, or shaped. Cornbread, loaves and dumplings are made from drop batters, while muffins and gingerbread are made from pour batters. Tea breads and coffee cakes are made from soft doughs, and biscuits can be made from either.

Sourdough baked goods

Although the breads are different, the ingredients are basically the same. The variety comes from the diversity of cereal products used: wheat, rye, and corn flours and bran, oatmeal, or cornmeal. Further variety comes from the way the dough or batter is shaped and cooked.

Capturing the kernel of Old West cooking, these batter and dough recipes bring back a special taste and texture that can not be bought in a store.

CHAPTER 2
True Grains
Batters and Doughs

DON'S FLAPJOHNS-SOURDOUGH FLAPJACKS

Don Getz of Salt Lake City suggests serving these yummy pancakes with lots of cowboy coffee and good syrup. You can fold in your favorite berries just before ladling the batter onto the griddle. Remember to save some of the starter for the next batch.

1 c. potato sourdough starter
1 c. flour
2 T. bacon grease, lard or shortening
½ c. condensed milk
1 tsp. baking soda
2 T. sugar
pinch of salt

Blend the ingredients. Allow to bubble for three to five minutes. Drop by the spoonful or ladleful onto a hot griddle. Warm maple syrup and melt butter for best toppings.

For starter: boil potatoes and save the water. Mix two cups of the water with enough flour to make a thick dough. Put this mixture into a crock and cover, but not too tightly. Set in a warm place for a few days to ferment. Store starter in refrigerator; it will keep about two weeks without using. Otherwise, store in the freezer.

FLANNEL CAKES

Call them flapjacks, hot cakes, wheat cakes, pancakes or flannel cakes, they are all griddle cakes. Flannel cake here implies a thick pancake made in plate size. Sometimes flannel cakes are made with a thin batter. Lyle Loban's grandmother sometimes served them with greengage syrup. Lyle still flips his flapjacks at his home in Yale, South Dakota

6 eggs, lightly beaten
2 lbs. flour, about 8 c.
½ gill yeast, about ¼ c.
1 tsp. salt
sufficient milk to make a thick batter, about 6 c.

Into the eggs, stir flour, yeast, salt and milk. Grease your griddle and heat it. Drop the batter by large spoonfuls; when bubbles appear, turn the cakes. Bake until golden brown. Butter them and send them hot to the table, commencing after the family is seated.

Make the flannel cakes at night for breakfast and at ten in the morning for tea. Store in a cool place.

WHOLE WHEAT WAFFLES

Bill Austin of Fort Madison, Iowa, suggests using only butter in these naturally good waffles. A word about waffle irons: The Scandinavians, with their "edelskiver" probably made the most waffles in the Old West.

2 eggs
1¾ c. milk
½ c. butter, melted
1 c. whole wheat flour
1 c. all-purpose flour
4 tsp. baking powder
1 T. sugar
½ tsp. salt

Preheat the waffle iron. Beat eggs until light and fluffy. Add milk and butter, mixing well. Beat in combined dry ingredients, mixing until just blended. Pour batter onto center of hot waffle iron. Bake until steaming stops about 5 minutes. Remove from waffle iron, and serve the way you like 'em.

BUCKWHEAT PANCAKES

Buckwheat pancakes were an excellent way to start the day in the Old West. Buckwheat is fading from our diets, but you can bring it back by making these pancakes.

3 c. water, lukewarm
2 T. molasses
4½ tsp. dry yeast or
  2 small pkgs. cake yeast
2 c. buckwheat flour
1 c. whole-wheat flour
½ tsp. baking soda
½ tsp. salt
1 T. drippings, plus
  more for greasing
  the griddle
brown sugar, optional

The night before serving, put ½ cup of lukewarm water in the bowl and stir in molasses. Add the yeast, and stir in 2 cups more warm water and both the flours. Cover with a cloth and let stand at room temperature to make the sponge.

Next morning remove 1 cup of the sponge to a jar as a starter for the next batch. Store in refrigerator. Dissolve baking soda and salt in ½ cup of hot water and add drippings. Beat this into the sponge until well mixed. Heat the greased griddle. Pour the batter and cook until bubbles form and burst; then turn and cook on the other side. If you sprinkle each cake with a little brown sugar when stacking, they'll taste even better.

Keep the starter in the refrigerator. For the next batch, make the sponge by mixing the starter with 2 T. molasses, 2 c. "bloodwarm" water, 1½ c. buckwheat flour, and 1 c. whole-wheat flour. Let stand overnight, then proceed as before, setting aside a new cup before adding final ingredients.

GRIDDLE CAKES

From an old scrapbook of recipes belonging to her mother, who passed away in 1912, Eunice Christian of Yellville, Arkansas, offers this recipe for griddle cakes:

2 c. sour milk
1 tsp. salt
3 c. flour
1 tsp. soda
1 c. boiling water

Beat and let stand overnight the milk, salt, and flour. In the morning dissolve the soda in the water and mix with the other three ingredients. Bake on hot griddle, with plenty of grease.

SWEET DUMPLINGS

As a variation from griddlecakes, with the same ingredients and some syrup, the cook could prepare dumplings in syrup for a sweet treat. Mabel Bays of Tulsa, Oklahoma, sent a recipe for dumplings that can be cooked in real or imitation syrup, honey, or even a caramel sauce for dessert.

2 T. shortening or other fat	½ c. sugar, or less, if preferred
1⅓ c. flour	½ c. milk
2 tsp. baking powder	½ tsp. vanilla, optional

Mix the above ingredients. Drop dumplings into simmering syrup or sauce by heaping teaspoonful. Keep tightly covered. Cook on medium heat for 20 minutes. Let stand covered, several minutes after removing from heat. Serves four. Can be topped with cream.

GREEN CORN GRIDDLE CAKES

Vivian Turnbull of Battleground, Washington, still has a recipe for special pancakes made by her grandmother who came out from North Dakota in 1918. The recipe has been in the family since before the turn of the century.

2 eggs	1 tsp. baking powder
1 pt. milk	2 c. grated green corn
flour sufficient to make good batter	butter for serving and greasing
pinch or two of salt	

Beat eggs and milk. Add the dry ingredients and the corn. Fry on hot griddle. Butter them hot and serve.

BANNOCKS

As a boy Paul E. Brunner in 1915 camped in the mountains tending cattle. He and his fellow cowhands made bannocks for their bread. Paul still makes this recipe at his home in Valier, Montana.

2 lb. sack of flour	⅓ cup melted fat
1 c. sweet milk	
2 T. baking powder (Use 1 T. baking soda if milk is sour)	

Remove half the flour from the sack and set aside, leaving a hollow in the center of remaining flour. Stir milk, leavening, and fat together. Slowly pour this into the sack of flour hollowed out to half the amount. Slowly stir in the rest of the flour until quite thick. Then place the dough in a greased frying pan and set on top of the stove until done on the bottom. Flip over and bake on the other side.

GRIT BREAD

According to B. H. Roach of Oklahoma City, the Indians made grit bread when they camped. Roach's mother-in-law is Vinnie James Humes and his brother-in-law is Overton James, the present Chickasaw tribal governor.

Grate roasting ears on piece of tin punched with a nail and attached to an 8-inch wide board; or use the jaws of a deer. The milk from the grated corn will make a batter; salt and bake as you would cornbread.

PIONEER HOMINY

Grandfather Bunch made this hominy in 1854 when crossing the plains from Missouri to Oregon. His granddaughter Hattie E. Nevin, of Coquelle, Oregon, made it, too, for her husband and herself to eat in their log cabin.

2 or more qts. dry corn
  off the cob
2 gals. boiling water
2 level tsp. lye

½ lb. butter
2 c. cut-up salt pork
  or bacon
pepper and salt

Pour the corn into the water, to which lye has been added. Keep water and corn warm for 12 hours. Keep hands out of the lye water! Drain lye water off corn. Rinse well in warm water 3 times. Rub corn between hands until all loose corn covering shell has come off. Place corn in hot water. Add seasonings and butter with the pork. Cook about 10 to 12 hours until tender and well done.

Cornmeal Corner

BOILED INDIAN BREAD

Edith Schiller, of Montana, whose pie recipes you'll love, says that baked beans were a staple of the washday diet. With the beans, her mother served this bread, which Edith remembers as a special treat after school on a cold, wintry day.

1 qt. sour milk
1 qt. cornmeal
1 pt. flour
1 small teacup molasses,
  about ¾ measuring cup

1 tsp. salt, optional
1 tsp. saleratus (soda)

Mix everything. Put in a three quart pail and cover tightly. Put in a kettle on a support and cover with water. Boil for 4 hours. You can also bake this bread covered in the oven on low heat, 300° for about 3 hours.

CUSH

La Verne E. Ray of Yuba City, California, remembers an old family recipe similar to bread soup, but made with corn bread. Sometimes cush is crumbled corn bread fried up in butter or fat. This version is cooked in boiling water.

1 pt. crumbs
butter, the size of an egg

boiling water
salt and pepper

Crumble corn bread; to each pint of crumbs add butter the size of an egg. Pour in hot water until it is the consistency of gravy. Season liberally.

CORNMEAL BATTER CAKES

Harriet Davis still makes these in Oregon. We have a few more of her delicious recipes throughout the book.

Into a quart of sour milk, stir in a tablespoon of soda; beat in 5 eggs, a teaspoon or two of salt, and as much cornmeal as will make a stiff batter. Bake on a griddle, like buckwheat cakes.

SKILLET CORN BREAD

Bill Lantz of Rialto, California, has cooked this bread over a campfire, on a barbecue grill or atop the stove.

1 c. cornmeal
1 c. flour
  sifted for lighter product
½ tsp. salt
1 tsp. baking powder

1 c. milk
1 egg, beaten
½ c. vegetable oil
  or melted bacon grease

Mix dry ingredients well. Stir in the rest. Pour into heated skillet on top of stove or campfire. Cover skillet and cook 20 to 30 minutes.

Savor the aroma and serve with butter and honey.

CORN PONE

In 1860 the grandmother of Harriet Davis, Phoenix, Oregon, used this recipe for corn pone:

Pour 6 cups boiling water over 3 pints of sifted cornmeal and beat it to a batter with a wooden spoon. Add 2 teaspoons salt. Let stand until cool; then put it into a tray and work well with hands, adding 2 quarts of dry sifted cornmeal, until it is pretty stiff.

Have your Dutch oven very clean and well buttered; warm it through, and fill it more than half full. Set it in a warm place, and let it stand 12 hours. In that time the corn pone will sweeten and become light.

When ready to bake, put oven over bright coals; heat the top of the oven on the fire, and when you place it on the oven, cover it with coals. Let the corn pone bake slowly and when done, set it by and let it cool in the oven.

This bread cannot be baked in anything but a Dutch oven or deep skillet with a cover. If baked in any other it would not or could not be corn pone. But it might still be corn pone if you put your Dutch oven or cast iron skillet inside your electric or gas oven to bake.

ORANGE CRACKLIN' BREAD

To a basic corn bread recipe add orange juice to replace the milk, plus one tablespoon of grated orange peel. After mixing the dry ingredients, add the orange juice and egg at the same time. Add cracklings, or leave out to make plain orange cornbread.

SCRAPPLE

Cornmeal was used in making scrapple, a hearty breakfast dish in Pennsylvania, and in southern states such as Tennessee and Kentucky. Many westering immigrants came from those state and continued cooking scrapple in their new homes, even in the Northwest. John Norwood of Arvada, Colorado, has been making scrapple over half a century.

Take scraps of pork, part of the heart, neck bones, etc., and boil until meat slips from bones. Chop fine. Set aside the liquid used in cooking the meat until it cools. Remove the cake of fat from the surface.

Return liquid to a fire and bring to boil. Add meat and season to taste with salt, black pepper, a bit of cayenne and a touch of sage. Let it boil again. Then reduce to a simmering heat and thicken with cornmeal, white for rich folks and yellow for "pore" folks, just as in making cornmeal mush. Stir carefully or the mush will spatter you with hot globules.

Cook about one hour stirring constantly at first. If boiling becomes to fast, remove from fire, stir and return to stove at simmering.

When done, pour into a large pan to cool and mold. When cold, slice in half-inch thickness and fry brown in bacon grease. Turn frequently to be sure it doesn't burn. Serve Yankee style with maple syrup or Southern style with sorghum.

SAUSAGE SCRAPPLE

Instead of adding pieces of meat to the cornmeal, Ruth Mast, Parma, Idaho, adds sausage. This scrapple was eaten hot at night with a bit of sweetening or fried for breakfast.

1 c. cornmeal
5 c. boiling water
½ tsp. black pepper
½ tsp. sage
½ tsp. poultry seasoning
1 lb. sausage, broken into small pieces, and cooked until lightly browned

Stir cornmeal into water in a double boiler or a heavy pan. Add pepper, sage and poultry seasoning. Stir the sausage into the cornmeal mush. Cook the scrapple 1½ hours over low heat, covered.

Pour the scrapple into containers or bread pans rinsed with cold water. Cover with a wrap. Let stand overnight. Store in a cool place, so that it will harden and not crumble when fried.

Unmold; slice in ¾ inch slices, and fry in hot grease until browned. Serve with syrup, jelly or honey.

ARKANSAS CORN BREAD

"We eat lots of corn bread in Arkansas," says Mrs. Lester Christian. We know they do, 'specially in Ozark country—with lots of dark greens and hog products.

1 c. cornmeal
1 c. flour
¼ c. sugar
4 tsp. baking powder
½ tsp. salt
¼ c. melted bacon grease, or fat for pan

Preheat oven to 450°. Grease bottom and sides of pan. Mix all ingredients together. Bake 20-25 minutes. Enjoy!

CRACKLIN' CORN BREAD

Ardis Shilton in Flat, Texas, remembers this special corn bread baked at hog butchering time when her mother cooked out the lard. She writes, "Daddy always wanted this bread made from the brown cracklings strained from the lard."

1 c. cornmeal
1 T. flour
1 tsp. soda
1 tsp. salt
1 c. sour milk
1 egg, unbeaten
1 c. cracklings

Combine all dry ingredients; mix well. Add milk and unbeaten egg; mix well. Add cracklings. Put a small amount of fat in a heavy 9 inch pan and let heat until really hot. Add mixture and bake.

CRACKLING BREAD

As more products became available, housewives could vary their corn bread. Some even substituted canned soup for part of the liquid. Lenora Taylor of Tahlequah, Oklahoma favors this recipe.

¾ c. cornmeal
¼ c. flour
1 tsp. soda, level measurement
½ tsp. salt
2 c. buttermilk
1 egg, optional
1 c. cracklings, "real crisp"
1 to 2 T. oil

Sift dry ingredients, add milk, egg, and cracklings. Place one or two tablespoons cooking oil in baking pan. When oil is hot add bread mixture to pan. Bake at 400° until golden brown on top.

CHICKEN OR TURKEY SPOONBREAD

In Tahlequah, Oklahoma, the spoonbread is special when Lenora Taylor puts chicken or turkey in it:

3 c. milk or a mixture of broth with milk
¾ c. cornmeal
2 or 3 eggs, separated
1 tsp. salt
1 tsp. baking powder
2 T. melted butter or oil
1 c. chopped chicken or turkey

Heat milk or mixture. Stir cornmeal into milk and cook until thick, about 5 minutes. Remove from heat and beat in egg yolks, one at a time. Stir in the salt, baking powder, butter, and chopped chicken or turkey. Fold in stiffly beaten egg whites. Turn into greased casserole or baking pan. It is best to have grease hot in pan when pouring the mixture into it. Bake 325° to 350° in oven till firm, about 30 minutes.

Lenora buys her cornmeal at a 146-year-old mill. She likes to top a meat pie with corn bread.

RYE N' INJUN

My Iowa born great-grandmother treasured this recipe. Cornmeal was often known as Injun meal. Anadama bread was another name for this rye, corn and molasses bread.

1½ c. rye flour
1½ c. yellow cornmeal
 (injun)
1 T. baking powder
3 eggs, separated
½ c. molasses or
 brown sugar
2 c. buttermilk
 more or less
½ c. melted butter,
 or lard drippings

Mix the dry ingredients. Beat in the egg yolks. Add enough molasses and buttermilk to form a thick batter. Beat well. Beat the egg whites until stiff and fold gently into the batter. Put into an oiled, heavy baking pan. Bake at 350° until a skewer comes out clean, about 35 to 45 minutes. Serve hot with butter.

BEAN AND ONION CORN BREAD

"When I was growing up, whether they be red, brown or white, beans were the main source of our diet," says Carolyn Stewart of Collinsville, Oklahoma. "They were good, filling and cheap. It seemed we always had some left over, but never enough for another meal, so Mamma made use of them by adding them to our corn bread." Carolyn and I know you'll like this one.

2 c. cornmeal
1 tsp. baking powder
pinch of salt and sugar
1½ c. buttermilk
2 eggs
1 small diced onion
about 2 c. leftover beans,
 drained, (or whatever you want
 to get rid of)

Mix the dry ingredients; then add the milk, eggs, onion and whatever amount of beans you have left over. Pour into a greased iron skillet and bake at 450° for 25 minutes, or until firm and brown on top.

CORNMEAL MUFFINS

Texan James Fury turns his cornmeal into muffins. In his mail order recipe business he has many tasty recipes, some of which he shares with us in this book. In the Old West, muffins were often called "gems."

2 c. cornmeal
1 c. boiling water
a dessert spoonful of
 lard, or 1 heaping
 tablespoon
1 tsp. salt
1 T. white sugar
1 pt. cold milk
2 eggs,
 well beaten
2 T. wheat flour
2 tsp. baking powder

Sift cornmeal into a bowl and scald well with water, beating the meal until perfectly smooth. Add lard, salt, sugar, milk and the eggs. Beat all into a smooth batter. Sift the flour and baking powder into the batter. Have muffin pan greased and heated. Half fill each compartment and bake in a good oven 350° from 30 to 35 minutes.

BUTTERMILK CORN BREAD

Frontier women were creative cooks with corn. The men may have liked to put their corn into whiskey, but they enjoyed when on their own frying up some skillet corn bread. A cast iron skillet cooks the most authentic corn bread.

Joe Teague was ninety-four years old when he contributed this recipe. It has served him well over his years in Dumas, Texas.

1 c. buttermilk
1 egg
1 tsp. baking powder
½ tsp. salt
½ tsp. soda
1 T. flour
2 c. cornmeal
¼ c. shortening or oil

Mix ingredients in order given, stirring enough to mix well. Put the shortening into a baking pan or an iron skillet. In the oven at 350°, or on top of the stove heat the shortening till melted and rather hot. Pour in batter and bake 30 minutes at 350° or until brown on top.

MEXICAN CORN BREAD

Nat Gibbs of Beaumont, Texas says that Mexican corn bread is "so good that you have to be driven away from the table with a buggy whip and run off the premises with dogs just so the wife and kids can have a little." Years ago his wife fell heir to this recipe that has been treasured and passed down from generation to generation, and ever since, he has "eaten so much of it that he has grown thin from toting it around."

Mexican corn bread was born in the scorching heat of the Texas border country, where the sun lies low and the dust devils dance. Later it made its way across the state and into the kitchens of East Texas where it found a warm welcome and decided to stay. Warning: it is a well known fact that Pancho Villa will come out of his grave and ride for miles to get a pone of this corn bread; so don't cook it up when the wind is blowing toward the South. It may carry the aroma and who knows, the old pistolero, himself, might ride up to your kitchen door.

1 can corn, cream style
1 c. yellow cornmeal
1 c. milk
2 eggs, well beaten
½ c. bacon drippings
8 oz. grated sharp cheddar cheese
½ tsp. baking soda
1 tsp. salt
1 lb. ground meat
1 medium size onion, chopped
4 jalapeno peppers, chopped

In a large mixing bowl combine the cream style corn, cornmeal, milk, eggs, bacon drippings, baking soda, and salt.

Brown the ground meat with the onions mixed in. Drain the mixture and add the jalapeno peppers. Mix well. Next, add the cheese and fold it in. Set the mixture aside.

Pour half of the batter mixture into an iron skillet. On top of this add the meat mixture. Then pour the remaining half of the batter mixture over the meat mixture. Put this into an oven and bake at 350° for 50 to 60 minutes.

MEAT PIE WITH CORN BREAD TOPPING

1 lb. ground beef or
 chopped, leftover beef
1 large onion, chopped
1 can tomato soup, 10 oz. size
2 c. water

¼ tsp. black or chilli pepper
1 c. kernel corn, drained
½ c. chopped green pepper or
 1 tsp. dried sweet bell pepper

Brown meat and onion in skillet. Add soup, water, pepper for seasoning (soup is already salty), corn and green pepper. Simmer for 15 minutes. While meat mixture is simmering, prepare corn bread topping as follows:

¾ c. cornmeal
1 T. flour
1 T. sugar
1 tsp. baking powder

1 egg, beaten
⅓ c. milk
1 T. cooking oil

Mix corn bread ingredients. Place meat mixture in bottom of casserole; leave large space on top for meal mixture. Pour meal mixture on top of meat mixture. Bake 350° until brown.

Rise 'N Shine With Yeast Breads

MISSION LOAVES

2 c. whole wheat flour
 plus more as needed
3 c. water
½ c. oil or fat
1 c. honey
2 T. yeast

½ tsp. salt
1 c. yellow cornmeal
1 c. cracked wheat
1 c. yam or substitute
 vegetable, grated

The foods of early California relied on corn. Later other grains were harvested to make mission loaves which were cooked in beehive ovens near the mission cookhouse.

Into a large glass, pottery or wooden bowl put the flour, water, oil, honey, yeast, and salt. Stir well and let sit until spongy. The time will vary depending on the weather. Yeast acts more slowly in cool weather.

When the mixture is bubbling, add the cornmeal and the cracked wheat plus the yam, pumpkin, yellow squash, or carrot. Stir well. Add more whole wheat flour to prevent sticking.

When well-kneaded, form into one large or two smaller loaves and put onto oiled baking sheets. Make diagonal slits in the top to prevent cracking. Leave until almost double in bulk and bake in a moderate oven, 350° for about 1 hour, depending on the size of the loaf. It will sound hollow when tapped on the top if done.

When done, paint all the surfaces with butter or other fat and wrap in a clean cloth and leave until cool. This makes a tender crust that will slice well. The bread will keep at least a week and freezes well.

DAISY'S OATMEAL BREAD

Oats are the easiest grains to grow in a climate where the temperatures dip. Daisy Leist of Fargo, North Dakota, where the farmers needed all the energy provided by the oats, knows her oats about making bread. It makes good horse sense to make this oatmeal bread.

1½ c. boiling water
1 c. rolled oats
1 tsp. salt
⅓ c. light molasses
1½ T. shortening (melted)
 or cooking oil

1 pkg. dry yeast
¼ c. warm water
4-4½ c. flour, sifted

Pour the boiling water over the oatmeal. Add the salt and molasses. Stir and cool to lukewarm. Add oil and yeast dissolved in the warm water to the oatmeal mixture. Gradually add the sifted flour until the dough is stiff enough to handle. Knead the dough on a lightly floured board for about 5 minutes, or until dough is smooth and elastic.

Place dough in lightly greased or oiled bowl, turning to coat all sides. Cover with a clean cloth and let rise in a warm place until double in bulk.

Punch down the dough and knead again for a few minutes. Shape into a loaf and put in a well greased or oiled 9 x 5 loaf or in smaller pans. Cover and let rise again, about 1 hour, until double in bulk.

Bake at 375° for 50 minutes. Remove bread from pan, brush top crust with oil or grease and cool.

CHEECHAKO BREAD

With enough starter to keep the yeast working, this is a fast rising bread. Walt Thayer, of Wenatchee, Washington, says it originated with the gold rush to Alaska. The name means **newcomer** or **beginner.**

1 pkg. yeast
1 c. water
1 T. sugar
1½ c. sourdough starter
 use recipe in this chapter

1 to 2 tsp. salt
3 c. flour,
 plus 1 to 2 cups more

Stir the yeast, water, sugar, and starter together. Then add the salt and 3 cups flour. Stir well about 5 minutes longer. Dough will be sticky and may look lumpy. Cover with a damp cloth and let rise 1-1½ hours in a warm place. Turn dough onto a floured board and work in 1-2 cups of flour until dough is no longer sticky. Knead until satiny and shape into one or two loaves. Slash top of loaves diagonally. Let rise 1-1½ hours; then bake 40 to 50 minutes in a preheated oven at 400°. Cool on rack.

Serve thick slices to your family. Walt says they'll holler for more if you serve the bread with lots of homemade butter or fresh honey. Pure maple syrup is also good as a topping.

SALT-RISING BREAD

This is one of those recipes that uses your kitchen know-how as you go along. Mrs. Don Swank got it from her mother-in-law, Elizabeth Swank. Use a very well-greased or buttered pan, since there is no fat in the recipe. Any extra batter can be used for pancakes and waffles.

1½ qt. lukewarm water
1 T. sugar
1 tsp. salt
6 c. flour for sponge, then more
 for bread, about 9 cups in all

Mix the water, salt and enough flour, about 6 cups, to make a batter, not too thick. Let stand until it has fermented and is foamy. A warm place is best.

Put some more flour, about 3 cups, in a pan. Pour in your batter with a little more water, if necessary. Mix well. Let stand until it rises and then make into 2 loaves and let it rise again.

Bake about 45 minutes at 350°. The bread will rise more while baking. It might stink a little while baking, but it tastes all right.

RAILROAD YEAST

Judy Michaels found this rare recipe in a century-old cookbook. Use 1 teaspoon to a baking of salt-rising bread, to aid in fermenting or as a booster in any recipe, along with the yeast.

1 T. ginger
1 tsp. soda
1 pt. of boiling water
coarse flour or middlings—
 any commodity of an
 intermediate grade, about ½ cup

To the ginger, soda, and water add the flour to thicken. Let it rise, and set in a cool place.

HOMEMADE YEAST

Harriet Davis of Oregon has a recipe for extending the yeast supply.

a handful of hops
3 pts. water
1 pt. flour
1 c. yeast
½ c. molasses
pinch of salt

Boil the hops in the water for half an hour. Remove from the heat and strain half the water over the flour. Mix it well, and pour on the rest of the water. When it is almost cool, add the yeast, molasses, and some salt.

CHUCK WAGON SOURDOUGH STARTER

In a 1962 True West letter to the editor, Buttermilk Smith, alias Milt Hinkle, gave this recipe for sourdough starter.

To make sourdough, you need an earthenware crock, one gallon size. Dissolve one cake of yeast in one quart warm water, add three tablespoons of sugar, one quart of sifted flour. Mix well and let set until mixture is light and slightly aged (thirty to forty hours). Do not let it get too sour and don't let the sponge chill.

POTATO YEAST

Harriet Davis has also made yeast from potatoes.

a handful of hops	1 pt. flour
2 qts. water	2 T. salt
several cooked potatoes	1 pt. brewer's yeast

Boil the hops in the water for half an hour. Strain the water from the hops on the potatoes. Mix the flour and salt with the potato mixture. When it is lukewarm, add the brewer's yeast, and let it stand 6 hours to rise.

Strain it through a colander and put it into an appropriate container for storage. The yeast will keep a week in summer and longer in winter. Refrigerated, of course, it will keep longer.

BASIC RANCH HOUSE BREAD

Sourdough was the mainstay of many pioneers' and prospectors' bread products. Melissa Blankenship's sourdough traveled to the Oregon-California trail, and her recipe still survives.

Mix 1 cup flour with 1½ cups water or milk and leave in a glass, ceramic or plastic container, uncovered, until it begins to bubble. Depending on weather and climate, this will take from 48 hours to a week. Stir every so often to keep from crusting over. You can cheat by adding one tablespoon of active dry yeast.

Now for the bread: Place starter in large bowl. Add 2 cups flour and 2 cups milk or water. Let it set until spongy. Replenish starter in crock, leaving about 2 cups in bowl. To this add 2 or 3 T. oil, melted butter or drippings. Add enough flour to make into a soft, kneadable dough, about 3 cups. Knead well, but do not work in too much flour.

When dough is smooth and elastic, put in an oiled bowl and let rise until double in bulk. Punch down and knead again. Form into large round loaf and set on oiled baking pan to rise. When loaf has risen, make cross design in top with sharp knife. Paint with lightly beaten egg white and put in oven at 450° for about 5 minutes; then reduce the heat to 350° and bake for 40 to 45 minutes or until hollow sounding when tapped. For a crisp crust, paint the loaf with melted butter, wrap in clean cloth and leave to cool.

Your sourdough can be used for lots of baked goods—cookies, cakes, muffins, and, naturally, biscuits.

BUTTERED BISCUIT

Biscuits made with yeast and lots of butter are especially good the way Harriet Davis, of Phoenix, Oregon makes them!

1 lb. butter, softened	½ pt. yeast
2 lbs. flour	1 T. salt
1 qt. warm water	

Work the butter into the flour; moisten with warm water and good yeast, plus salt; work it very hard until it is smooth and light. Bake in a brisk heat, about 425°. This makes a lot of biscuits but you can use some of it for the top crust of a pot pie.

ALASKA SOURDOUGH STARTER

"We men have culinary skills, too!" says Michael Eugene Daniels of Anchorage, Alaska. His recipe for sourdough starter is a favorite with old sourdoughs in our forty-ninth state. The starter is great for pancakes, breads, cakes, etc.

2 c. flour	1 pkg. active dry yeast
3 T. sugar	2 c. warm water (105°-115°)
1 tsp. salt	

Whip the ingredients gently with a whisk until well combined. Cover loosely with plastic wrap, waxed paper, or a damp towel and let stand at room temperature for 3 days, stirring daily.

At the end of 3 days, starter should be bubbly when stirring it and have a clean, sour, somewhat alcoholic aroma. The starter is now ready for use. To replenish after using, add 1 cup flour, 1 cup milk, and 1½ cup sugar. The starter can be stored in the refrigerator for up to 14 days.

ICEBOX SOURDOUGH BISCUITS

5 c. flour	1 or 2 pkg. Fleischmann's dry yeast in 1 c. warm water
¼ c. sugar	
2 tsp. salt	2 c. buttermilk
4 tsp. baking powder	½ c. melted shortening
½ tsp. baking soda	

Mix well all ingredients. Put in a crock or glass container with tight fitting lid (foil works well) and put in refrigerator. Leave for at least 12 hours. Use as desired. Knead lightly on a floured board. (If dough is soft use a little extra flour.) Wedge or cut out biscuits. Place in greased pan and let rise for one hour or more. If you want the biscuits to rise extra high, pack tight in a high sided pan. Bake at 350° for 20 minutes or until brown. This dough will keep in refrigerator about 8 or 10 days. If kept longer it will not rise.

SOURDOUGH BISCUITS

½ recipe for Basic Ranchhouse Bread	butter bits, lard or other fat
1 tsp. baking soda	oil or drippings

Add the soda to the bread dough. Knead as directed. Roll out to ½ inch thick. Dot the top with bits of butter, lard or other fat. Fold in half, roll and dot the surface again. Fold and roll once more, this time leaving the dough about 1 inch thick. Cut into rounds with a 2 or 3 inch biscuit cutter. Place on an oiled baking sheet and paint tops and sides with oil or drippings. Let set until well risen and bake at 350° for 20 to 25 minutes.

COWBOY BISCUITS

Cowpunchers in their chuck wagon cooking favored biscuits of several types. For 12 to 16 biscuits follow this recipe:

2 c. starter	1 tsp. baking soda
½ c. milk	2 T. melted fat
½ T. sugar or honey	2½ to 4 c. flour
½ tsp. salt	

For dinner biscuits, "set" your starter at breakfast; for breakfast biscuits, set your starter the evening before. Do this by adding 2 cups each of flour and warm water to the starter in crock. Stir well and let it ferment all day or all night.

Mix starter with milk, sugar, salt, baking soda, and fat. If starter is thin, omit milk. Blend well, then work in enough flour to make a soft dough, between 2½ to 4 cups. Knead lightly. Pinch off dough balls and roll into biscuits. Place together in a well-greased pan and turn over so greased sides are on top. Let rise in a warm place for about 45 minutes; then bake in a 375° oven for 30 minutes, or until biscuits are done.

For skillet sourdough bread, fry the dough as a flat bread.

Or, to make the bisuits in a Dutch oven:

Dig and fire the Dutch oven hole. Generously grease the Dutch oven and let it warm. Put biscuits in Dutch oven with sides just touching. Replace lid. Make a hole in the hot coals and shovel about an inch of dirt over the coals. Put Dutch oven into hole. Put hot coals on the lid. In 15 minutes the biscuits should be cooked.

For Dough Sticks: Wrap the dough around a stick in a spiral shape. Cook over a camp fire.

Quick Breads

BISHOP'S BREAD

The story behind this quick bread made with nuts and fruits is that the bishop called unexpectedly on a pioneer family one afternoon. The surprised housewife wanted to serve him something special; so she used what she had at hand, proving again that necessity is the mother of invention.

2 c. flour	4 eggs, beaten
1 tsp. baking powder	½ c. honey
1 tsp. baking soda	½ c. buttermilk
½ c. chopped dried figs	⅓ c. melted butter
½ c. chopped dates	1 T. herb, such as
½ c. chopped nuts	yarrow—optional
½ c. dried mixed fruit	

Preheat oven to 325°. Stir together flour, baking powder, and baking soda in a large bowl. Stir in fruits and nuts. In a small bowl, beat eggs, honey, buttermilk, butter, and herb. Add to flour mixture. Stir well and turn into a greased and floured loaf pan. Bake for 1½ hours until the top is golden and a pick inserted in the center comes out clean.

Cool in pan for 10 minutes. Remove from pan, wrap well and store for 24 hours before slicing. But if you wish, you can slice it after briefly cooling.

ACORN BREAD

Acorns were the staff of life for some Indian tribes.

1 c. acorn meal
½ c. cornmeal
½ c. whole wheat flour
½ tsp. salt
1 T. baking powder

3 T. salad oil
½ c. honey
1 egg
1 c. milk

Combine acorn meal, cornmeal, flour, salt, and baking powder. Stir until well blended. In another bowl, combine salad oil, honey, egg, and milk. Add to dry ingredients and mix just until all ingredients are moistened. Pour into greased 8-inch square pan and bake at 350° for 20 to 25 minutes. Cut into thick slices and spread with butter.

QUICK LOAF BREAD

Here's a real "bare-bones" recipe for a quick bread from Waldo Olson, of Omaha, Nebraska.

4 c. flour
2 T. plus 1 tsp. baking powder
1 T. sugar
1 tsp. salt

a potato, boiled, cooled and peeled
milk or water
2 T. butter

Sift together flour, baking powder, sugar, and salt. Into these rub one medium sized potato. Add enough milk—if your cow is dry use water—to mix smoothly into a good, stiff batter. Place in a well-greased loaf pan and smooth top over with a buttered knife; stand pan in warm place about a half hour. Then bake in 350° oven about one hour. When baked, moisten top crust with damp cloth. Remove from pan, wrap and allow to cool.

HUCKDUMMY

One of the foods that Will James missed as a trapper/trader was huckdummy. It's a quick bread with raisins. Add 1 cup of raisins and about 2 cups of milk or water to the quick bread recipe.

OATMEAL MUFFINS

To preserve his grandmother's 1875 original recipe with its distinctive oatmeal flavor, Don Getz never adds berries or nuts to the muffins.

1 c. all-purpose flour
⅓ c. sugar
¼ tsp. salt
2 tsp. baking powder
1 tsp. cinnamon

1 c. uncooked oats
3 T. melted lard or oil
1 egg, beaten
1 c. milk

In a large bowl, mix together flour, sugar, salt, baking powder, oats, and cinnamon. Mix in the oil, egg, and milk; stir until dry ingredients are well moistened.

Spoon into a well greased muffin tin or paper muffin cups set in the tin and bake at 425° for 15 minutes or until tops of muffins are browned, and a wooden pick inserted in one comes out clean.

BREAD SOUP

Edith Scholey of Prescott, Arizona, tells an interesting tale of her grandfather's love for bread soup. "My grandfather, Jim Foster, worked for many years on Verde River ranches in Arizona, a few miles south of what is now Clarksdale, where I spent summers with him and grandmother. He was of Irish descent and very definite about everything. The ranches produced superb fruit, but he rarely ate any. Every evening meal had to start with bread soup, a simple but delicious dish. Grandmother only made one bowl, just for him, but I tasted his many times." Edith always serves the bread soup to anyone in her family who is ill. Another name for this is Graveyard Stew.

2 slices bread cut
  in 1-inch squares
butter, about ½ square or
  rectangle, or bacon fat

2 c. whole milk
pepper and salt

Melt butter in skillet until sizzling hot. Toss bread in butter until browned nicely on all sides. Do not soak bread in butter. Add more butter if needed, but skillet should be quite dry. Add milk; bring to a boil, and pour into a bowl. Then sprinkle with seasoning but do not stir. This can be held up to ½ an hour. Makes 1-2 servings.

FLOUR TORTILLAS

Tortillas replaced the yeast bread the mountain men missed. Those wintering in Taos, Santa Fe and some California settlements learned to love this chewy bread, which the natives taught them to make.

3 c. unsifted flour
2 tsp. baking powder
¾ tsp. salt
about 1 c. warm water

Sift dry ingredients together. Gradually stir in water until a crumbly dough is formed. Work the dough with hand until it sticks together. Put on a board and continue kneading until smooth and elastic. Divide into about 10 pieces and roll each between palms to form balls. Let rest a few minutes. Then one at a time flatten the ball and roll out to 6 or 8 inches, rolling from center to sides and keeping as nearly circular as possible. The rounds should be about 1/8 inch. Stack them up until ready to bake.

Bake on a dry medium hot griddle. The tortilla will bubble; press down with a flat spatula, turn and bake other side. Repeat until surfaces show golden brown at the bubbles.

Soak a towel in warm water and wring out as dry as possible. As each griddle of tortillas is done, stack them on half the damp towel and fold the other half over them. Continue until all tortillas are baked; then place stack and towel in bag.

The corn tortilla is crisp; the flour tortillas should be capable of being folded to scoop up foods.

Mexican and New Mexican were among the people driving wagons in the West. They used their Dutch ovens for spicy stews and their skillets to make tortillas.

NAVAJO FRY BREAD

Serve this bread hot as a snack or with any main dish.

2 c. white flour
1 tsp. baking powder
½ tsp. salt
water enough to make a soft dough
1 c. lard for frying

Mix all ingredients, except lard, and knead until the dough is soft and elastic. Pinch off pieces about the size of a walnut and roll out on floured board until ¼ inch thick. Make a small hole in the center of each round.

Melt 1 cup lard or heat 1 cup oil in a heavy skillet. One at a time, place the dough rounds into the hot fat and fry until brown and crisp. For another version of Navajo Fry Bread, try this:

2 c. flour
2 c. dry milk
2 tsp. double-acting baking powder
¼ tsp. salt
1 T. lard, cut into small bits plus 1 lb. for deep frying
½ c. ice water

Combine flour, milk, baking powder, and salt and sift into a deep bowl. Add lard bits. With fingertips rub the flour and fat together until the mixture resembles flakes of coarse meal. Pour in water and toss ingredients until the dough can be gathered into a ball. Drape the bowl with a towel and let the dough stand for about two hours.

After two hours, cut the dough into three equal pieces. On a lightly floured surface roll each piece into a circle about eight inches in diameter and 1/4 inch thick. With a knife cut two four-or five-inch long parallel slits completely through the dough, down the center of each round, spacing the slits about one inch apart.

In a sturdy skillet, melt lard over moderate heat until it is hot. The lard should be about one inch deep in skillet. Fry the breads one at a time for about two minutes on each side, turning them once with tongs. The bread should puff slightly and become crisp and brown. Drain the bread and serve warm. It's good with honey.

SOPAIPILLAS

4 c. sifted flour
1½ tsp. salt
1 tsp. baking powder
1 T. shortening
1½ c. warm water (approximately)

Combine dry ingredients and cut in shortening. Make a well in center of dry ingredients; add water and work into dough, adding only enough water to make a firm dough. Knead dough 15 to 20 times and set aside for approximately 10 minutes. Roll dough to 1/8 inch thickness or slightly thinner; then cut in squares or triangles—do not re-roll any of the dough. Cover the cut dough with a towel as you fry the sopaipillas in very hot fat (420°). The sopaipillas should puff very soon after being dropped into the deep hot fat. Fry only a few at a time. Drain sopaipillas on absorbent toweling and serve as a bread with any Southwestern meal. They are especially good served with honey.

Sopaipillas may be dusted with a sugar-cinnamon mixture and served as a dessert with New Mexican Chocolate. Stuff hot sopaipillas with frijoles refritos, chile con carne, chopped onion and grated cheese for a luncheon dish.

Thanks to Mrs. Lillian Lopez of San Bernadino, California for this recipe.

VANISHING VITTLES

Whatever happened to pease porridge? Hasty pudding? Son-of-a-gun-in-a-sack? Many Old West recipes are extinct but some have changed with the times and are still enjoyed today.

Hardworking pioneers started their day with plenty of calories. Along with meat, eggs, sausage, and pie, there was mush and syrup. In times of crop failure there may have been just mush, gruel, or porridge, which were varieties of hot cereal. Porridge was often made with oatmeal but sometimes included other grains and vegetables. *The Little House on the Prairie* books mention bean porridges being served for supper. Gruel was simply a thinner version of porridge.

Pudding, a much broader term than porridge, is used to describe a wide variety of food. There are baked, boiled or steamed puddings, savory and sweet puddings, hot or cold puddings, and puddings served as main dishes, side dishes, or desserts.

The two chief types of puddings are the cereal based dishes and suet dishes. The cereal based puddings, with a texture resembling custard, were originally boiled or baked. Suet dishes such as plum pudding were boiled in a bag. Son-of-a-gun-in-a-sack swelled when prepared in a kettle. The sack took the place of sausage casing, holding the ingredients together.

Sweet dessert puddings are more modern than the non-sweetened varieties. When sugar became more widely available in the late eighteenth and early nineteenth centuries sweet pudding became more common. Americans inherited their pudding cookery from the English. They used native ingredients to build upon the English foundation. When the English wheat flour was not available, settlers used cornmeal or a mixture known as rye 'n Injun (a mixture of rye flour and cornmeal).

Like the heart, however, the palate is unchanging. Let's go home again to the Old West with some fine old puddings and porridges.

CHAPTER 3
Puddings and Porridges

(Some hot. . .some cold. . .some in the pot nine days old.)

LUMPY DICK

Much "guess, gosh, and know how" went into the Old West recipes. T. D. Church of Bellvue, Washington, knows when the weather got bad the old cow gave little milk and the chickens laid only an occasional egg. Those were the times for Lumpy Dick.

1 egg
¾ c. flour
2½ c. milk
salt, optional
sweetener

Break egg into flour. Stir with a fork until lumpy. Add just enough milk to make a pourable mixture, but leave the lumps. Add salt, if desired. In a kettle, bring the remaining milk to a boil and add the egg mixture. Cook for 15 minutes or until a toothpick inserted into the center comes out clean.

Serve the Lumpy Dick in sauce dishes with the rest of the milk and a "bit of sweetener" such as honey, molasses or sugar. The housewife had the satisfaction of knowing she had divided one egg equally among her entire family.

HASTY PUDDING

Puddings commonly were made in a Dutch oven with cornmeal or leftover bread and spruced up with whatever else was on hand. These dessert puddings, though, weren't as simple as Hasty Pudding or cornmeal mush. This recipe was one of the first to appear in the brand new cookery column in *True West*, February, 1983. Note that you can use degermed cornmeal. The cornmeal with the germ intact, however, can be obtained at a health store, a mill, a gourmet store, or a food co-op.

1 c. yellow cornmeal, preferably with germ not removed. (Degermed cornmeal has had the nutritious fiber removed.) The pudding will still taste as good without it.

4 c. cold water, plus ½ tsp. salt
butter

In a bowl combine the cornmeal and one cup cold water. In a Dutch oven or heavy saucepan bring remaining water and salt to a boil. Carefully stir in the cornmeal mixture, making sure it does not lump. Cook over low heat stirring occasionally, for 10 to 15 minutes. Serve pudding with a pat of butter and one or more of these toppings: Maple syrup, brown sugar, molasses, or light cream.

SON-OF-A-GUN-IN-A-SACK

This pudding was a favorite on the range. When the cook wanted to be nice to the cowhands he made it. Raisins or dried apples and suet were added to a soft pudding. The mixture was placed in sackcloth and boiled in a big kettle of water or Dutch oven until done. The fact that it was so much trouble to make probably gave it its name. It has a coarser alias. This recipe accompanied Barbara Blackburn's first story for *True West*, "Cooking with a Dutch Oven," Feb., 1983.

2 c. flour
½ c. sugar
1½ c. soft bread crumbs
1 T. baking soda
1 tsp. ground cinnamon
¼ tsp. ground cloves
¼ tsp. ground nutmeg
1 c. raisins, chopped dried apples
 or prunes or combination thereof
1 c. ground suet or sausage meat
½ c. chopped nuts
1 can evaporated milk,
 or ⅔ c. light cream
 or buttermilk
½ c. molasses
sweetened cream, optional for
 topping

In mixing bowl combine first seven ingredients; add raisins, suet, and nuts. Stir in milk and molasses. Mix well. Arrange layers of cheesecloth to form a 16-inch square, about 1/8 inch thick and set it in a 1 quart bowl. Fill cheesecloth with pudding mixture. Bring up sides, allow room for expansion and tie tightly with string. (If you have equipment for plum pudding, use that.) Place the "sack" in a colander. Place colander in kettle and add enough boiling water to cover the sack. Cover and boil gently for two hours. Remove colander; remove cheesecloth from pudding at once. Turn pudding rounded side up on plate. Let cool for about 30 minutes before serving. This can be refrigerated. Served cold, it is agreeable, but it is best re-heated. Reheat in a 325° oven, covered or wrapped, till warm.

GRAHAM PORRIDGE

Puddings and porridges prepared from cornmeal, wheat, oats and other grains were sometimes served for breakfast, other times dessert, and—when the cupboard was bare—as the main course. This recipe comes from James Fury of Brownwood, Texas.

3 c. boiling water
½ tsp. salt
⅓ pt. graham flour or
 whole wheat flour
cream and sugar

To the boiling water add the salt and gradually stir in the graham flour by the handful. Let it boil thoroughly after each addition of flour, so that it is kept constantly boiling. Serve with cream and sugar.

For a smoother porridge add the flour to cool water and stir all ingredients. Bring to a boil and continue boiling until thick enough to serve.

Chill any leftover porridge. Cut it up into squares and fry it up in fat for supper's dessert or next morning's breakfast.

PEASE PORRIDGE

Many little houses on the prairie served porridge made of peas and beans. In the four-part series for *True West* Barbara Blackburn used the recipes in "Forgotten Frontier Foods."

6 c. water	½ tsp. pepper
1 lb. dry green split peas, washed	1 c. sorrel and/or spinach
¼ lb. salt pork	1 tsp. dried mint leaves
1 c. chopped onion	2 T. butter
½ tsp. marjoram	

In a Dutch oven or similar vessel, put water, peas, salt pork, onion, marjoram and pepper. Bring to a boil and simmer for about an hour until the peas are almost tender.

Remove the pork and save. Mash peas or leave them as they are. Add the chopped greens and mint and simmer for about 15 minutes.

In the meantime, chop the salt pork into bits and fry or bake in a hot oven, 425°. Top the porridge with bits of butter and pork.

MISSION CORN PUDDING

This was a favorite at the missions in early California. In an article for *Old West*, Summer, 1983, Geraldine Duncann gave this recipe.

1 c. cornmeal	1 T. sugar
1 c. boiling water	2 T. drippings
1 tsp. baking powder	2 c. milk
½ tsp. salt	4 eggs, separated
1 can of whole kernel corn drained or the equivalent in fresh corn cut from the cob	

Heat oven to 375°. Put the cornmeal in a large mixing bowl and add boiling water, stirring until the meal is thoroughly blended. Add all remaining ingredients except egg whites and beat well. Beat egg whites until stiff and gently fold into batter. Pour into a well-oiled casserole and bake 45-60 minutes or until firm and a delicate brown. Serve immediately, spooned right out of the casserole. The pudding will fall some as it cools.

CHAMPURRADO

Southwesterners use chocolate to make breakfast porridge.

6 T. grated chocolate	2 eggs, well beaten
6 T. sugar	2 tsp. vanilla
1 c. hot water	sprinkling of cinnamon
5 c. hot milk	
½ c. masa harina (browned for better flavor	

In a double boiler, combine the chocolate and sugar. Slowly add the hot water, stirring until a paste is formed. Slowly add the milk, then the masa harina which has been thinned with a little of the hot liquid. Before serving, fold in the eggs, vanilla and cinnamon. Serves about 5.

Time for Pumpkin Pudding.

PIMA PUMPKIN PUDDING

The original Indian-influenced pudding from the Southwest was probably more basic; today's Indians make this mouth-watering variation.

3 c. cooked pumpkin
1½ c. brown sugar
1 tsp. cinnamon
1 tsp. ground ginger
1 c. rich milk or
  light cream
4 eggs, separated

To cooked pumpkin add brown sugar, cinnamon, and powdered ginger. Mix well. Add milk and the egg yolks.

Beat the egg whites until stiff and gently fold them into pumpkin mixture. Pour into well-oiled baking pan and bake at 350° until a toothpick or knife inserted into the middle comes out clean. Serve immediately with cream.

INDIAN MEAL PUDDING

Another version of Indian Pudding can be cooked on top the stove. Martha Sutton, Russell Springs, Kentucky, says this recipe is dated circa 1850.

3 pt. sweet milk
2 apples, chopped fine
1 c. cornmeal
½ c. granulated sugar
½ c. blackstrap molasses
1 lb. raisins, more or less
1 pinch salt

Put two pints of the milk into a pan over boiling water in a double boiler. Add the apples and the cornmeal. When well scalded add the sugar, molasses, salt to taste, raisins, and (lastly) stir in the last of the milk. Cover and cook over low heat until the pudding is thickened to your taste.

FRUITED INDIAN PUDDING

What makes this Oklahoma Indian Pudding from Lenora Taylor different from the Northeast version is the dried fruit.

1 qt. milk
½ c. cornmeal
1 c. molasses
1 tsp. salt, optional
1 c. peaches, dried
1 c. raisins

Scald milk, add cornmeal and cook in double boiler 15 minutes. Add remaining ingredients and pour into greased 1½-2 qt. baking dish. Bake at 300° for three hours, or until firm in the center.

BAKED INDIAN PUDDING

In his grandmother's 1892 cookbook, Lyle Loban of Yale, South Dakota, found this recipe using Indian meal.

1½ qts. scalded milk
dash salt
½ c. Indian meal or yellow corn meal
1 T. ginger
1 c. molasses
2 eggs beaten or 1 tsp. saleratus (baking soda)
1 T. butter or "piece the size of a common walnut"

Let the milk, meal, salt, and ginger stand for 20 minutes. Add the molasses, eggs or soda and the butter. Bake two hours at 325°.

SPOTTED PUP

The cowboys loved this raisin rice pudding. And who wouldn't?

½ c. uncooked rice
½ c. sugar
½ tsp. salt, optional
½ tsp. ground nutmeg
2 qt. milk
¾ c. raisins

Mix rice, sugar, salt, and nutmeg in a shallow 2½ qt. baking dish. Add 1 quart of the milk. Then, to prevent spilling, add second quart of milk after placing dish in the oven. Bake in preheated 325° oven for 2½ hours, stirring twice during first hour. Stir the brown crust into pudding several times during the remainder of baking time. Add raisins 30 minutes before pudding is done. Then allow crust to form again. Serve with cream, if desired.

You can also cook rice pudding on top of the stove. Use cooked rice and 1½ quarts of milk.

WAGON TRAIL CORN

Corn, grits and water make a soup to eat on or off the trail. The family of Lenora Taylor of Tahlequah, Oklahoma cooked this soup.

Parch corn in hot ashes until brown. Sift the ashes out of the corn and heat until a grit stage is reached. Sift the meal until nothing but the grits are left. Add the grits to hot water to make a soup to suit your taste.

POOR MAN'S SOUP

Julia Mathisen, great-grandmother of Irene Pecoraro of Lander, Wyoming, pushed a hand cart from St. Joseph, Missouri to Kamas, Utah on the Emigrant Trail in 1866. This was one of her recipes that has been handed down through the family.

Fry several pieces of bacon, adding ½ cup of raw chopped onions, 2 cups of raw diced potatoes and saute until golden brown. Then add enough flour to make a thin gravy, stirring constantly; so it won't lump. Then add water and stir well until well heated. Season to taste with pepper and salt, and you will have a pot of "poor man's soup" that will stick to your ribs and satisfy your hunger, when your cupboard is low on groceries.

GRANDMA'S GRUEL

Anna Kuhlman of Marshfield, Missouri remembers her grandmother's southern gruel.

broth from a ham bone
4 T. cornmeal
1 c. onions, finely diced

Sprinkle the meal into the boiling broth to thicken. Add the onions, and heat slowly for ten minutes or until thick enough for soup. Add salt and pepper.

CAST IRON COOKERY

The West was won with hot iron. Dutch ovens for soups and stews were found at the hearth and over the campfire. Besides Dutch ovens, a well-equipped chuck wagon had several three-legged skillets or spiders. Those utensils lasted a long time. If another was needed, it could be purchased at the general store.

Cast iron cookware is still popular. Many authentic Western cooks insist on it. It is not mandatory, however, to cook the recipes in this chapter with cast iron.

Early pots were available only in cast iron or expensive copper or brass. When tinware appeared in the U. S. it was accepted because of its light weight. The tin peddler often exchanged his wares for the price of the peddler's non-perishable product. In 1883 a tin spice box cost 75¢.

In the late 1850s a new alloy called Britannia was developed. It looked like pewter but had a more silvery sheen and could be silverplated.

Iron cookware returned to popularity during the late 1800s and early 1900s. The porcelain enameled cast iron utensils were inexpensive and sturdy. Available in speckled blue or grey, agate iron was also popular at the turn of the century. Its mottled design resembled the mineral it was named for.

Once she had her homestead in order, gadgets for every task were available to the homemaker. Among the simplest and most useful mechanical devices was the eggbeater. Earlier cooks used a fork, wire whisk, narrow-slotted wooden paddle, or small broom. By the end of the century beaters were made with tin blades and iron cranks and handles.

Soups and stews cooked in iron were more nutritious because the broth became literally iron-enriched. In recipes for soups the term bouillon and broth are often used interchangeably. Stew in a strict sense means food cooked slowly in a liquid in a covered pot. In the Old West, that pot was usually a cast iron Dutch iron.

38 — Old West Cookbook

CHAPTER 4
Soups and Stews
Protein In A Pot

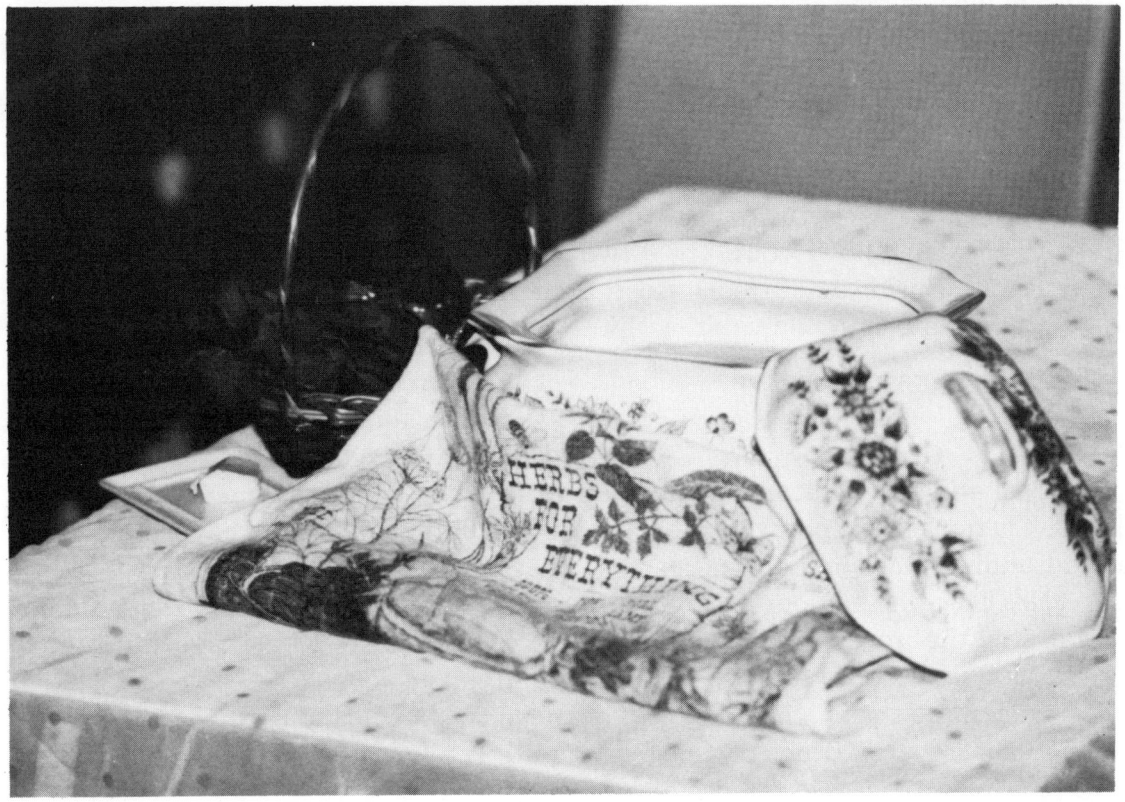

Sorrel Soup

SIMPLE SORREL SOUP

What is a weed today may have been food to our ancestors. As more Americans become more health conscious, they are returning to nature's larder. Not well known today, a hundred years ago, the pleasant acidic flavor of this spinach-like herb was valued in soups and salads. Its vitamin C content helped prevent scurvy and other diseases. Although cultivated sorrel is best, wild sheep sorrel will do in a pinch. (Sorrel has come out of hiding and can be found in the gourmet produce section of large supermarkets.)

2 c. sorrel leaves
1 c. water
1 c. milk
2 T. butter

Finely chop the fresh sorrel leaves. Add the water and simmer ten minutes, then puree at high speed in a blender or force through a food mill. Add milk and butter. Mix thoroughly, season and serve hot.

GRANDMA'S BEAN SOUP

Eunice Christian of Yellville, Arkansas found an 1890 cookbook in a box of junk at an auction. This was one of the starred recipes.

1 lb. navy beans
1 ham bone or 2 hocks
2 tsp. salt
½ tsp. pepper
1 bay leaf crushed
2 onions sliced and browned
2 finely diced carrots

Soak beans overnight. Drain, cover with water and add other ingredients. Cook till tender. You may have to add more water.

CHEESE AND POTATO SOUP

When the near-zero temperatures prevailed and supplies were short, this Midwest meal-in-a-bowl would thaw two moderately congealed people and warm them from the inside out. Mrs. H. Rose, Westport, Connecticut, believes the recipe to be Amish in origin.

2 to 3 large potatoes, cut up
2 T. flour
3 T. butter
1 medium onion, diced
½ to 1 c. longhorn cheese, diced
vinegar to taste

Peel and boil potatoes. Drain the tubers when they are done and save the liquid. Then mash the potatoes well, gradually adding the water they were boiled in and adding more liquid if necessary. Season to taste.

Next brown the flour and butter by stirring constantly until a rich golden brown. Add the browned mixture to the potatoes and stir the whole savory solution as you boil it together for two or three minutes.

Distribute the onion and cheese between the bowls and pour the soup over them. Sprinkle a few drops of vinegar over all. If you are serving more than two or three people, increase the recipe.

TASH PASHOFA

B. H. Roach of Oklahoma City, Oklahoma tells us that "Tash" is the first part of the word, "Tanchi," or corn, and "Pashofa" is for the cracked corn the Chickasaw Indians prepared.

3 lb. corn
2 gal. water
3 lb. fresh pork

Bring water to a brisk boil; add corn which has been soaked overnight, slowly into the boiling water. Cook over slow fire, stirring often to keep from scorching. Add meat to corn while the corn is still firm. Each individual salts to his own taste. Cook until meat is tender and soup thick. More water may be added while cooking to maintain its soup consistency. This dish is especially good served with corn grit bread and wild onions.

ONION AND NASTURTIUM SOUP

¼ c. unsalted butter
4 c. spring onions, thinly sliced
3 T. flour
2 c. favorite chicken stock
2 c. plus 2 T. milk
1/8 tsp. white pepper
2 c. nasturtium leaves (Grow your own or beg some from a friend!)

Melt butter over medium heat. When foam subsides, add onions; saute until wilted. Reduce heat to low; cover pan. Sweat onions until tender, about 10 minutes. Sprinkle flour over onions; cook, stirring constantly 2 minutes.

Heat stock, 2 cups milk and pepper in medium saucepan to simmering. Gradually whisk stock mix into onion mixture in large pan. Simmer, about 20 minutes, stirring occasionally. Puree in sieve, or go modern and use a blender.

Plunge nasturtium leaves into a pan of simmering water. Cook 30 seconds; drain. Combine with 2 T. milk and puree till smooth. Add cream; blend. Swirl this into the other soup. Ladle soup into bowls. Top with flowers, various colors for different bowls.

(The recipes for both sorrel and nasturtium soup come from *Herbs From A To Z and a Pot of Tea*, 1981, by Barbara Blackburn, self-published, by Circulation Services.)

APACHE ACORN STEW

Savory stews can be made from creatures that gallop, fly, swim, or even from one that just falls from a tree. It is one of the few remaining authentic Apache dishes. Many Apache housewives try to gather at least 100 pounds of acorns every autumn so they will be able to satisfy their family's hunger for this favorite meal.

This recipe from Carolyn Niethammer of the Southwest is made easier if you follow the directions of Euell Gibbons for grinding acorns into meal.

1 lb. beef stew meat, cut into chunks
water
½ c. acorn meal, finely ground
seasonings

Place stewing beef in a heavy pan and add water to cover. Simmer until beef is very tender and falling apart. Remove beef from liquid and chop into very fine pieces. Return meat to liquid. Stir in acorn meal, salt and pepper to taste. Heat.

ACCORDING TO EUELL GIBBONS:

Put acorns and hot water in an electric blender, turn it on high speed and let it hum until the acorns are finely ground.

Put the acorn meal in a piece of cloth and press out the water, add more hot water; squeeze that out, and keep doing this until the squeezed-out water loses its tea color and becomes clear.

VICTORY SOUP

When Davilla Bright's mother moved from Alabama to Midliothian, East Texas, the nearest larger town was Waxahachie. Her Uncle Tom rode horseback into Waxahachie one day and had lunch at a little restaurant named Victory. He had very little money, but found a Victory special—a bowl of soup and crackers for a nickel. He ordered it hoping it wouldn't be too tasteless and thin. To his surprise the soup was delicious. Uncle Tom enjoyed the soup so much that he told his mother and sister about it, when he reached home that night, hoping that they would make some in the future. They did, and even today the present members of that family include Victory Soup among their favorite dishes. If fresh blackeyed peas are used the soup should be simmered for at least an hour; leftover ingredients do not require as much cooking.

1 soup bone	okra
tomatoes	onions
blackeyed peas with water in which they were soaked or canned (There should be twice as much liquid as vegetables in the soup.)	potatoes

Be sure that fresh blackeyed peas are soaked overnight or boiled for two minutes and left for an hour to soak before adding them to the water and the soup bone. Add enough liquid to make the quantity of soup you plan to serve.

Combine soup bone, tomatoes, peas, okra, onions, and potatoes. Bring to a boil, and then simmer until the vegetables are tender.

BEEF, BEANS AND BEER

In her Western Publications article about steam beer in old San Francisco, Geraldine Duncann included a recipe for using beer in her stew.

2 c. dried red or pinto beans	1 bell pepper, cut in strips
1 lb. beef	1 c. molasses
1 large onion, cut into rings	1 tsp. mixed herbs
6 to 8 cloves of garlic, peeled and crushed	1 T. chili powder
½ small chili pepper or ½ tsp. crushed chilies	¼ tsp. cumin seeds or ¼ tsp. ground cumin
2 or 3 stalks celery, diced	ale or steam beer

Cook the beans until tender. Drain and put into an ovenproof dish with a tight lid.

Cut inexpensive beef into thin strips and saute in drippings until browned. Add beef and remaining ingredients except beer to the beans. Stir gently and add enough brown ale or steam beer (plain American beer may be substituted) to come to one thumb knuckle above the level of the beans in the pot. Cover and bake at 350° until the liquid is almost gone. You may need to remove the lid part way to allow for evaporation of some of the liquid. Taste for seasonings. Serve hot with corn bread.

WEBSTER'S CHOWDER

Daniel Webster was famous for the excellence of his chowder. His 100-year-old recipe was submitted by Judy Michaels, of Yacaipa, California, who makes the soup for a local Hilton. Unless you're cooking for a ship, cut the recipe in half.

4 T. chopped onions fried with one slice of bacon
1 qt. well-mashed potatoes
1½ lb. ship biscuit or crackers, broken
1 tsp. thyme
½ bottle of mushroom catsup or ½ c. catsup and ½ c. mushrooms
1 bottle claret or port wine
½ grated nutmeg
few cloves, mace, allspice
slices of lemon
black pepper to taste
6 lb. blue or white fish, cut in slices
25 oysters shucked
1 c. cornmeal, optional

Put everything in a pot and cover with an inch of water. Cook slowly and stir gently. When done to your taste, stir in one cup of cornmeal to thicken. You may have to add additional water unless you like your chowder super thick; of course, you may leave out the cornmeal.

BEEF GUMBO

Gumbo, a well-seasoned dish made with seafood, poultry, meat, vegetables, and always okra, is a good example of what can be done with simple ingredients. The search for an herb starting with "U" inspired the unicorn pods to replace the okra. The recipe comes from Barbara Blackburn's *Herbs From A To Z and a Pot of Tea*.

2 T. butter
soup bone with about 3 lb. meat

In a Dutch oven melt the butter. Add a soup bone and saute until golden brown. Pour in 2 to 3 quarts of water and simmer with the following for two hours.

¼ c. chopped celery
¼ c. minced parsley
¼ c. chopped onion
¼ tsp. paprika

Strain, cool and skim the stock. Melt 2 more tablespoons butter. Add the following and saute for three minutes:

½ c. chopped onion
1 c. sliced okra or unicorn plant pods

Add and simmer for an hour longer:
meat removed from bone and chopped
2½ c. chopped tomatoes
1 T. sugar
soup stock, with ½ c. reserved

Combine 1 T. file powder with the stock reserved. Add to the simmering soup and stir until combined. Makes about ten cups.

CHUCK WAGON STEW WITH DUMPLINGS

You can cook this stew without dumplings; otherwise, use the dumplings recipe in the chapter on batter and dough.

2 lb. stew meat, cut into 1-2 inch chunks	3 potatoes, cut into bite-size pieces
4 T. flour or cornmeal	2 stalks celery, with leaves thickly sliced
¼ tsp. pepper other seasonings to taste	2 carrots, sliced
1 lb. can tomatoes or equivalent fresh	2 c. cooked beans of your choice
2 onions	1 T. chili powder, optional

Dredge meat in flour and brown in fat in a heavy skillet or Dutch oven. Season with whatever herbs you want. Add tomatoes, onions, potatoes, celery, and carrots. Simmer slowly for 1½ hours. Add beans, then dumplings. Cook covered without lifting the lid for 15 minutes.

Covered Wagon Stew

SON OF A BITCH STEW

Follow recipe for Dutch Oven Stew in this chapter, but include the following items:

½ c. diced suet
½ lb. beef heart sauteed in suet
½ lb. fresh tongue, skinned and diced
½ lb. brains separated and floured and briefly sauteed in suet

1 marrow gut
½ lb. beef liver, diced and sauteed in suet
½ lb. sweetbreads, separated and floured and briefly sauteed in suet

(You may vary the increments according to the number of people you are serving.)

POET'S SON OF A BITCH STEW

If you like your stew recipe set to verse, here is an original from Don Getz.

Go get yourself a good-sized pot;
Fill half with water, not a lot.
Make a good fire, not too big,
Then set a grate for this stew-pot gig.
Be sure there's plenty of fire embers,
'Cause this here stew's good in September.
But if there's anything about stew you fear,
The Son of a bitch is good anytime of the year.
And the ingredients that you will need,
Are as follows for the cooking deed.

Unless told otherwise, measures are half-cups,
So do not bother with any ante-ups.
Peas an' carrots an' beans an' taters,
Corn an' okra and a can of tomaters.
Two pounds of beef cut in small hunks,
For more flavor add some bacon chunks.
Sprinkle in pepper and two pinches of salt,
A dash of tobasco and another, then halt.
Bring the whole mess to a rolling boil,
To make it look greasy add a dash of cook's oil.
Add all of the above to pot on the "fahr."
Sit down, rest easy and strum yer guitar.
Check out the lid so as not too tight,
To let the steam out into the cool night.
Check the pot for no overboil,
Don't waste good stew on Nature's soil.
Then after about an hour or two,
You can serve your hot Son of a bitch Stew.
When you serve it and want down-home taste,
Put it into tin plates so there's no waste.
Instead of crackers use sheepherder's bread,
Use if for soppings or stew as a spread.
After you've eaten it belch with delight—
The Son of a bitch Stew should be just right!

HOBO STEW OR JUNGLE STEW

Says Walt Thayer, now settled in Washington, "We never measured anything. Just took an equal amount of assorted vegetables and put them in a kettle or large can and added water and set it over the campfire to cook slowly until done. We added salt to taste and also bits of meat if available, and when it was done it was a thick, tasty soup. Not that diluted stuff you get nowadays! And if a hobo happened to 'appropriate' a stray chicken that came snooping around the 'jungle,' that added 'flavor' to the stew. The feathers were burned and the feet, head and guts were buried (for safety's sake) as the standard fine for stealing chickens was 30 days in the nearest 'Cross-Bar Hotel.' Anyway, the cooking cans may have been blackened on the outside, but the rule of the road was to leave them clean for the next man."

DUTCH OVEN STEW

A lover of old cast iron cookware, Bill Lantz of Rialto, California, owns 54 pieces, mostly different shapes and sizes. Bill and his wife Barbara prefer the Griswald or Wagner skillets. For them, "It's the only way to go!" One of his favorite recipes for his Dutch oven is this stew:

2 T. oil
2 lb. cut up beef
4 T. flour
2 onions
1 potato
2 carrots
1 qt. home canned tomatoes
vegetables of your choice;
  celery, corn, peas—
  suit your fancy
½ tsp. dried parsley
salt, optional
2 bay leaves
pinch oregano

Brown floured beef in oil with cut up onions. Cook a few minutes. Add vegetables and tomatoes; stir well and add spices. Simmer 3 hours, stirring occasionally. No water is required; the juice in the tomatoes should be enough moisture for a rich sauce. You can cook this stew indoors or outdoors.

LOGGER'S STEW

Hattie Nevin learned to cook for logging camps when she was a teenager. Her father owned and operated logging camps and her mother occasionally was camp cook. Every week Hattie made this stew—in larger quantities.

Fill a large kettle 3/4 full of water and add the following:

2 lb. or more beef cut
  into 1½-inch pieces
3 medium size onions, diced
4 large potatoes,
  cut into 2-inch chunks
4 medium carrots, sliced
1 stalk of celery, cut into pieces
3 turnips, cut into 1-inch pieces
seasonings to taste

Boil slowly until all ingredients are done. Add water as needed as stew boils. In a smaller pan, melt ½ c. butter and 4 heaping T. flour. Add some of the stew liquid and stir until smooth. Add to the stew to thicken. Serve with baking powder biscuits or garlic bread. If you're feeding a whole logging camp you'll have to increase the recipe!

EL PUCHERO (MEAT AND VEGETABLE STEW)

Here is an Old West stew with a south-of-the-border influence.

1 split knuckle-bone,
  sheep shank, or pig's foot
2 to 3 lb. larger than bite-size
  pieces of beef or pork
½ c. each partially cooked red,
  white and garbonzo beans
2 ears fresh corn,
  broken into pieces
2 medium yams
3 whole onions or 2 dozen
  whole boiling onions
2 or 3 whole sweet chilies

2 whole bell peppers
1 small hot chili
1 lb. broad beans or string beans
½ lb. raw pumpkin
  peeled and cut in chunks
1 or 2 whole tart apples
1 hard pear
6 or 8 teeth of garlic
1 or 2 leeks, if available
  cut into 4-inch lengths
  including most of the greens

In a heavy cast iron or earthenware pot with a tight fitting lid, lay all the ingredients in order. Pour over enough liquid—perhaps a mixture of ⅔ stock and ⅓ sherry—to come only about ½ of the way up the pot. Add a bouquet garni and a sprinkling of salt, if desired, and cracked black pepper to the top. Cover and cook slowly, about 325° in the oven for about 4 hours.

To serve, carefully lift out the meat and place in a tureen; strain broth and pour over the meat. Sprinkle liberally with chopped parsley. Serve hot with fresh steamy tortillas or mission corn pudding.

MULLIGAN STEW

Mrs. Lester Christian of Yellville, Arkansas, recommends a recipe from the pages of an old yellowed cookbook belonging to her mother. Recipes then left much room for improvising with optional ingredients.

Mrs. Christian's mother probably had an herb garden and would rely on the fresh herbs in season and the dried ones at other times. Although she didn't always write them in her recipe, you can be sure that she used them. Herbs and spices improve this stew much more than the salt shaker.

1 lb. lean meat
4 potatoes
2 onions
any other vegetable

Chop the meat fine. Cover meat with water and boil until it is tender. In the meantime chop the potatoes and onions fine, along with the other vegetable. Add these vegetables to the tender meat and cook until done, about 30 minutes. Season to your taste.

BASIC CHILI

If you know beans about chili, you know that chili doesn't have any! Mrs. Helen Grainger, of Laurel, Montana, knows her Mexican chili. Her mother, Lena Stouffer, was a child when she rode by covered wagon from Kentucky to Socorro, New Mexico in the late 1880s with her parents, the Reids. Raised among the Mexican people and their culture, she learned their cooking and language. When making the family favorite, chili, she never measured, just tasted and added. You can adjust this recipe to taste, and serve beans as a side dish. You can make your chili very rich by boiling soup and marrow bones ahead.

2 lb. beef in inch chunks, usually with some fat
2 medium onions or one large, cut up
2 medium cloves of garlic, optional
1 large can whole tomatoes
1 small can tomato paste, about 4 oz.
1 or 2 T. chili powder
salt and pepper to taste, optional
½ c. yellow cornmeal
additional tomato puree if needed or tomato paste and water

In large stainless steel or iron cooking pot, cover beef chunks with water plus two inches over. Simmer until beef is tender. Add the onion and garlic, then the tomatoes, mashed or cut up, with their juice, and the tomato paste. Simmer for a few minutes, stirring well. Add the chili powder, salt and pepper and check for taste after a while. Simmer for an hour or two and taste; meat should shred easily. Then brown the cornmeal in a skillet, and add it slowly to the chili, stirring well until it cooks to desired thickness, in about half an hour. (Try not to burn the cornmeal!) Add more liquid if needed. Enjoy the flavor of the meat and seasonings without the beans.

Chili Fixins'

CHILI WITH BEANS

Don Getz, of sourdough fame, knows how to make good chili, but he uses beans and ground meat. Use a fairly large kettle.

4½ lb. lean, ground beef, coarsely ground
2-16 oz. each cans whole tomatoes or 4-8 oz. cans juice and all OR fresh tomatoes
4 T. finely ground red-hot chili, more or less
4 T. finely ground mild red chili
1½ tsp. ground or crumbled dried oregano
2 tsp. ground dried cumin
½ tsp. ground cayenne
2 jalapeno peppers, seeds removed, finely chopped
2 cans red chili beans or pinto beans, or cook up your own, dried beans to make 32 oz.
8 oz. can tomato paste
½ masa flour, cornmeal, cracker meal or high gluten flour (used by chefs)
¼ c. water
salt, optional

Cook the meat and the tomatoes until the meat has lost its redness. Then add ground spices and salt. Bring to a boil and cook for about 15 minutes. Turn heat down and allow to simmer until large bubbles come to the surface. Add more liquid as needed to prevent mixture from becoming too heavy. Taste for seasoning. Add 1 or 2 jalapenos. Never cover the kettle while cooking, but stir often to prevent sticking to bottom of kettle.

About 2 hours before serving, add beans, tomato paste, and masa flour mixed with water to form a thin paste. Cook for another 30 minutes, stirring often. Then ladle up.

To add a little extra zest to the chili, you may want to add toppings such as chopped fresh onions, chopped green chili peppers, grated Monterey Jack cheese, and dairy sour cream. Garnish with parsley, and serve with corn chips or tortillas.

NEW MEXICO CHILI CON CARNE

Naomi M. Wood of Dover, Arkansas, says "Bah" to any chili with tomatoes. She moved to Socorro County by covered wagon, when the county still reached from east of the Rio Grande to the Arizona line. From memories of her meals with Mexican friends here is a recipe for meat with pepper.

3 lb. tallow (rendered out beef fat)
2 lb. beef, goat, or mutton, chopped small or ground coarsely
1 tsp. salt
½ tsp. black pepper
4 or 5 long pods of the hot red peppers, crushed with seeds removed
4 c. water

In a large cast iron pot, Dutch oven, or stainless steel pot melt the tallow and add the meat; brown. Then add the salt, pepper, chilies, and water. Bring to a boil; then reduce heat, and simmer until the meat is very tender, about one hour. Add more water if needed during the cooking time.

Serve with tortillas or crackers.

CHILI VERDE (or Speedy Gonzales Chili)

Green chilies go into this chili recipe from John Morrie of Fort Madison, Iowa.

2 lbs. beef, lean and coarsely ground
1 can, #2½ tomatoes
1 can 15 oz. tomato sauce
1 can 4 oz. green chilies, hot, whole
¾ tsp. cumin, ground
1 tsp. oregano, ground
¾ tsp. garlic powder
⅓ c. masa harina (corn flour from Quaker Oats Company) or cornmeal
2 T. paprika
1 tsp. New Mexico ground chili
salt to taste
2 cans, 15½ oz. pinto beans in plain sauce
1 can, #2½, water (Use the tomato can for the measure.)

Brown meat. Add tomatoes, sauce, both cans of chilies, cumin, oregano and garlic. Simmer for 15 minutes. Blend in masa, paprika and ground chili. Add the beans, their sauce or liquid and water. Stir until it all thickens, then simmer a few minutes.

PIGGIE STEW WITH CORN DUMPLINGS

If garlic prevents colds and wards off vampires, this stew will keep you healthy and safe! Simple country foods like this usually have hearty gourmet flavor.

1, 2 or 3 lb. pork butt roast, cut into bite-sized chunks
3 onions
10 cloves whole garlic, peeled
2 or 3 sweet peppers cut into large chunks
1 dozen onions, peeled
2 c. fresh, frozen or canned corn
1 c. pre-cooked lima beans
herb sprigs
1 T. sugar
salt and pepper
bouillon

Saute the meat in drippings until browned. Place the meat and all remaining ingredients in an ovenproof dish with a tight lid. Add a sprig of sage and thyme, sugar, salt and pepper to taste. Add enough stock or bouillon to cover. Cover and put in oven at 350° until meat is tender.

Dumplings

1 c. cornmeal
1 T. baking powder
3 eggs, separated
1 T. sugar
buttermilk
seasonings

Combine ingredients except egg whites and add enough buttermilk to make texture between a thick batter and a soft dough. Beat egg whites until stiff. Gently work in the egg whites. Remove lid from stew and cover with large spoonfuls of the corn batter. Replace the lid and continue cooking for another 30-45 minutes. Serve from the pot.

BEAN HOLE BEANS

Remember when you handle hot chilies to be careful. It's best to coat hands with cooking oil or wear gloves, and never touch your eyes.

1 lb. dry pinto beans	1 6-oz. can tomato paste
7 c. cold water	1 4-oz. can green chili peppers, chopped
2 lb. smoked ham hocks	
½ c. chopped onion	2 T. sugar

Rinse beans. Combine beans and water in Dutch oven. Bring to boiling. Simmer 2 minutes; remove from heat. Cover; let stand 1 hour. Or, add beans to water and soak overnight. Do not drain. Add ham hocks and onion. Cover; cook over low heat for 1 hour, stirring occasionally. Remove ham. Remove the meat from bones; dice. Return meat to beans. Add tomato paste, peppers, and sugar. Cover and cook till beans are tender, about 30 minutes more, stirring occasionally.

To make this dish authentic bury the bucket of beans in a hole full of hot ashes, dug near the fire. Keep the ashes hot. Cooking time takes a good part of a day.

RIBS AND DUMPLINGS

3 lb. beef short ribs, cut in serving-size pieces	1 16 oz. bottle of beer
salt and pepper to taste	1 chili pepper, seeded and chopped
1 medium size onion, wedged	1 T. vinegar
	2 T. sugar
1 clove garlic, minced	¼ tsp. nutmeg
1 large can tomatoes, cut	dumplings

Brown trimmed ribs in Dutch oven; season. Remove ribs. Drain off fat, reserving about 2 T. Add onion and garlic to reserved drippings; cook till tender. Add tomatoes, beer, chili pepper, vinegar, sugar, and nutmeg. Return meat to Dutch oven and bring to boil. Reduce heat; simmer, covered, till meat is tender 1½-2 hours. Cool; skim off fat. Return to heat; bring to boiling. Prepare dumplings (below). Drop batter by rounded teaspoons onto boiling stew mixture. Cover; simmer till dumplings are done. Don't peek for 10 minutes.

DUMPLINGS

1½ c. flour	salt and chili powder, optional
½ c. cornmeal	
4 tsp. baking powder	1 c. milk

Sift flour with cornmeal, baking powder, salt, and chili powder. Add the milk gradually, stirring.

HUNGARIAN PEPPER STEW

Hungarian pepper stew is big on flavor. This one comes from Tom R. Kovach, of Nevis, Minnesota. His dad, a Hungarian immigrant, came to America shortly after the turn of the century. Back then it wasn't the easiest thing to buy fresh tomatoes in the winter, so the tomato and green pepper part of it obviously made it a summer and fall dish.

4 medium potatoes
6 slices of bacon about 1/4 inch thick, cut into 1-inch pieces
1 large onion, diced
2 green bell peppers, diced
1 lb. stew meat, cut in 1-inch squares
2 whole tomatoes, wedged or 1 medium can tomatoes
1 small can tomato juice or 1 can tomato soup
paprika

Peel and boil diced potatoes until tender. In large skillet, fry bacon, adding onion. Add pepper along with the stew meat, slowly cooking until the meat is browned and almost tender. Add tomatoes and juice or soup and simmer until meat is tender. Season to taste and serve over the potatoes.

ESCALLOPED TURKEY CASSEROLE

Every so often the problem of what to do with chicken, duck, goose or turkey leftovers comes up. Will it be hash, sandwich meat—or what? This "or what" from the collection of Don Getz, Salt Lake City, Utah, dates back to 1910.

4 c. roasted or leftover turkey cut into bite-size pieces
6 T. fat drippings from roasted turkey
6 T. flour
4 c. hot turkey broth from giblets or chicken broth
1 c. soda cracker crumbs or cracker meal
paprika

Place the turkey chunks in a 9 x 13 pan or cake tin. Heat drippings, stir in flour and blend into a smooth paste. Remove pan from heat and slowly pour the hot liquid into the flour and fat mixture, stirring as you pour. Replace the pan over low heat and, stirring, bring to a boil; boil at least one minute. This makes a medium-thick gravy, use more fat and flour.

Cover turkey pieces with the gravy, top with the cracker crumbs or meal and lightly sprinkle with paprika. Bake at 400° for about 40 minutes or until cracker crumbs are golden brown. Mashed potatoes taste yummy with the gravy.

MENUDO

John Norwood contributed this recipe, once popular among trailblazers.

5 lb. tripe, sliced,
  or cut in oblong pieces or slivers
1 lb. beef or veal knuckle
5 or 6 cloves minced
  or pressed garlic
salt, optional
2 large onions, chopped
1 tsp. ground oregano
1 T. red chili powder
1 large green chili pepper
  seeded and chopped
1 large can drained
  golden hominy
2 T. lemon juice or tarragon
  vinegar
chopped greeen onions for a
  garnish

Boil the tripe and knuckle with other ingredients up to hominy in Dutch oven or large kettle with about a gallon of water to cover. Simmer about 5 or 6 hours until tripe is tender, adding water as necessary. Discard knuckle.

Add drained hominy. Bring to simmer and add lemon juice. Serve in a bowl with chopped green onions on top. Sprinkle with herbs to your taste. Serve with tortillas or other bread.

FISH STEW

Recipes from the Northwest often feature the fruits of the sea. To the Indians along the coast the catching, cooking and eating of salmon was a religious ritual. You can eliminate some of the seafood and substitute fish of your choice.

1/4 c. oil of your choice
1 c. chopped onions
1 c. chopped celery
1 T. garlic
½ tsp. thyme
½ tsp. grated orange peel
2 sprigs parsley
½ c. tomato paste
1 crumbled bay leaf
½ tsp. saffron, optional
1 qt. clam juice
2 c. dry white wine
2 c. chicken stock
1½ lb. halibut, cut in 2-inch
  pieces
1 lb. salmon, cut in 2-inch pieces
1 lb. cod, cut in 2-inch pieces
½ lb. shrimp
½ lb. crab, ready for cooking

Brown onions, celery and garlic in oil for five minutes, stirring constantly. Stir in thyme, peel, parsley, tomato paste, bay leaf, and saffron, if using. Pour in clam juice, wine, and chicken stock, and bring to a boil. Cover, reduce heat and simmer for 30 minutes. Strain contents to extract the juices. Discard the pulp.

Return stock to casserole and over high heat, bring to a boil. Drop in halibut, salmon and cod. Simmer for five minutes. Add shrimp and crabmeat. Simmer a few minutes until the fish flakes when prodded with a fork.

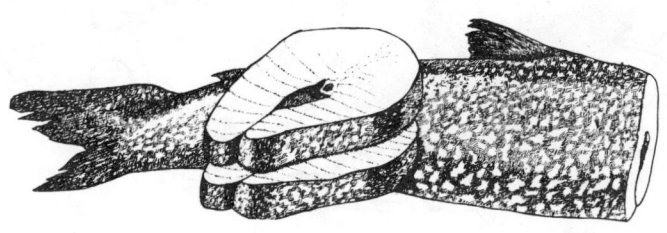

THE CALL OF THE WILD

When was the last time you had wild turkey, blackbird pie, or frizzled buffalo? Of all foods, it is wild meat that brings us closest to the pioneer's diet. Nature's gifts sustained many settlers and Indians. In frontier times, if you wanted food on the table, you had to shoot it.

When Great-grandpa was called for the midday meal, he might sit down to frizzled meat. That was shredded jerky, usually beef—possibly buffalo—fried till it curled and frizzled. Today we can buy chipped beef, but it has been smoked, not air-dried like the original version.

The meat that Great-grandpa preserved from his own hogs was salt pork. It was fried crisp and brown, and served with cream and biscuits. The pig also gave old-fashioned cooks lard to make flaky pie crusts and tender dumplings.

Holiday meals were real feasts. Wild turkey was often the main course. Goose was a specialty, perhaps stuffed with cornbread, and surrounded with a cranberry garland. Domesticated turkeys have replaced wild ones. Due to the difficulty and expense of confining and depinning geese, turkey is today's holiday bird.

We still eat chicken and dumplings, too, but not many of us kill "the old red rooster" when company comes. Abundant and economical, today's chickens are not for Sunday only. Their flavor, however, is not quite the same.

It was the good fortune of folks in the Old West to find the prairies alive with rabbits and prairie hens, the streams full of fish and the marshlands abundant with ducks and geese. It's our good fortune that some of their original recipes have survived.

CHAPTER 5
Field and Stream
Surf and Turf, Meat, Poultry, Fish

BUFFALO ROAST

The Indians and the settlers hunted and fished to provide food. Plains Indians, in particular, depended on buffalo as did West Coast Indians on salmon. Both foods were improved by the addition of herbs and berries. If you're game you may be able to find some meat for your recipe. Try the nearest buffalo farm—that's what I did!

1 c. apple cider and 1 c. red wine
½ c. red wine vinegar or
  cider vinegar
1 T. brown sugar
pinch of hot pepper
1 crumbled bay leaf
¼ tsp. chopped thyme or
  ¼ tsp. fresh (Always 3 times as
  much fresh or ⅓ less of dried)

1 onion, chopped
1 carrot, chopped
1 garlic clove, mashed
3 sprigs fresh parsley
8 peppercorns
6 juniper berries
1/8 tsp. each: chervil, tarragon,
  majoram
Whole filet of bison or
  rib buffalo roast, from 3 to 7 lbs.

In a heavy saucepan combine everything but the meat. Cook this marinade gently for 30 minutes. In the meantime wipe the meat dry with a damp cloth and put it in an enameled or porcelain dish or stainless steel casserole. Cover the meat with the marinade; then cover the dish. Keep it in a cool place from 24 to 48 hours, turning it occasionally.

Preheat the oven to 500°. Remove the meat from the marinade and reserve for basting. Wipe the meat dry; trim the excess fat, and tie if necessary, to hold its shape. Baste the meat at first with melted butter. Place it on a rack in shallow roasting pan. Roast in the middle of the oven for 20 minutes. Reduce heat to 350°. Baste with ½ cup of marinade; repeat every 15 minutes. Roast 16 minutes to the pound for rare, 18 for medium rare, 20 for medium and 26 for well-done.

Serve potatoes cooked in the roasting pan with the meat. Also good are tomatoes filled with creamed mushrooms, served with cress for edible garnish and a side of tart jelly.

BUFFALO JERKY

Remove all fat from a pound of buffalo meat. Freeze meat till icy. Cut in very thin strips, cutting across grain for crisp jerky and with grain for chewy. Place ½-inch thick layer in bowl. Sprinkle with salt, pepper, and liquid smoke. Repeat layers and seasonings. Weight down with plate or heavy object; cover. Chill overnight. Drain; pat dry. Arrange on rack in shallow baking pan. Bake at 250° till dry, 3½-4 hours. Cool. Store in airtight container in refrigerator or at cool room temperature. Makes 8-9 oz. This may not be exactly like the original, but it comes close.

BUFFALO TONGUE

The mainstay of the early West was less fatty and sweeter than beef. The tongue was a delicacy to the mountain men, and it was shipped back home to the East and to Europe. Much of the meat was made into jerky and pemmican. Homesteaders also prepared scrapple from buffalo meat. Pioneer immigrants traded with the Indians for buffalo and then dried it on the move. This recipe for buffalo tongue is a bit fancier than the covered wagon folks could prepare it:

1 buffalo tongue, but a
 cow tongue can be substituted
1 T. peppercorns and juniper
 berries to taste
2 laurel leaves

In heavy saucepan cover buffalo with water, peppercorns and juniper berries and laurel leaves. Boil two hours. Then slice thin and serve hot or cold, alone or with this sauce:

1 c. mayonnaise and yoghurt
 mixed
2 T. capers or
 pickled nasturtium pods
1 T. horseradish

1 tsp. oregano
1 tsp. parsley, sage
 rosemary and thyme, blended

Combine the ingredients and serve over the tongue. The mayonnaise cut with the yoghurt will make the low cholesterol buffalo even less fattening.

BUFFALO STEW

The Quarterly of the National Association often features recipes from Buffalo Jim Yapple. This is one of his.

2 lb. lean buffalo meat,
 cut into chunks
2 large onions, diced
1 c. tomato sauce
2 c. chopped tomatoes,
 including juice
1½ oz. beer

4 oz. chili mix
garlic powder to taste
cayenne, optional
cornflour
½ lb. Jack cheese, shredded
lime

Sear buffalo meat until brown. Throw in one diced onion and continue searing until onion is limp. Add tomato sauce and tomatoes. Stir well. Add the beer to the stew. Cook over medium heat until the stew is bubbling; then simmer gently for 15 to 30 minutes.

Add the chili and garlic powder. Add some cayenne, too if your like it hot. Heat to a boil, then cover. Simmer gently for one hour. Stir occasionally.

Add a little masa flour to some water to make a thin paste, then stir into the stew to thicken. Cover the pan and simmer gently for another half hour, stirring a few times.

Dish into bowls. Serve with the shredded cheese and lime.

GREEN PEPPERS WITH BUFFALO

This is another specialty of Buffalo Jim. He lives in California.

6 medium green peppers
1 lb. ground buffalo meat
1 medium onion, diced
1 clove garlic, minced

2 c. tomato sauce
1 c. cooked rice
salt and pepper, optional
½ lb. Longhorn cheese

Remove tops, seeds and membrane of peppers. Lightly sprinkle inside of pepper cups with salt and pepper. Cook peppers in boiling water for 5 minutes or steam for 10.

Brown the meat and onion in skillet with a little oil; then add garlic and tomato sauce and stir well. Add the cooked rice. Cover and simmer gently, stirring occasionally, for 20 minutes to blend the flavors. Fill the pepper cups with meat mixture just below the tops.

Cut the cheese into strips and stuff into the center of the pepper.

Place the peppers in a baking dish. Pour any extra filling around the peppers. Grate the remaining cheese and sprinkle over the tops of the peppers. Bake 20 minutes at 350°.

PEMMICAN

Pound dry lean meat (buffalo is best, but any meat such as beef will do) into a paste with fat. Add dried fruits, nuts, seeds, and herbs to taste, and press into cakes. The Indians sewed the pemmican into bags made from the buffalo hide.

ELK, VENISON, ANTELOPE, BEEF OR MUTTON TEXAS STYLE

Besides buffalo, other game included elk, venison, antelope, bear, quail, pheasant, and grouse. John Norwood has prepared these game recipes.

BRAISED BEAR

Bear steak
flour, salt, pepper, thyme
1 large onion, sliced
4 T. bacon grease

2 c. good stock or broth
1 c. dry red wine
½ c. tomato paste

Pound a bear steak, about 3 inches thick, with flour, salt, pepper, and thyme, using a heavy meat mall or hammer head. Brown onion slices in the bacon grease. Add the meat and brown well on all sides.

Mix stock and wine; bring to a boil and cook briskly for about 5 minutes. Turn the steak and push onions to sides of meat. Add about half the stock and wine and cover the pan. Simmer for about 1-1½ hours until meat is tender, adding more stock and wine, if necessary, so that it does not go dry. When steak is tender, remove to a hot platter. Add a half a cup of tomato paste and, if needed, addtional liquid to the pan juices to make a smooth sauce. Pour over steak. Serve with potatoes, parsley, and sauteed mushrooms.

TEXAS STYLE SWISS STEAK

Elk, venison, beef, or mutton
bacon grease
2 onions, thinly sliced
2 fresh green chilies
1 cup sliced, fresh mushrooms
1 T. flour
1 can beer
¼ each nutmeg, oregano, thyme
½ tsp. each black pepper and cumin
4 or 5 dashes tabasco
2 or 3 T. Worcestershire
1 tsp. chili powder
1 T. thinly sliced garlic
2 or 3 laurel leaves
1 small can tomato paste or 1½ cups canned tomatoes, drained

In a heavy skillet heat some bacon grease. Sear the meat in the hot grease till it is almost burnt on all surfaces and set it aside. Into the pan add the onions and green chilies or sweet peppers. When they begin to soften add the mushrooms. Saute until the onions are soft. Mix the flour into them and continue cooking until a light brown. Add a can of beer opened and let go stale. Stir and put the meat back in the skillet.

Mix the spices from nutmeg through laurel into the gravy given off by the ingredients into the pan. (The gravy is natural meat juice.)

Add a small can of tomato paste or 1½ cups canned tomatoes. Simmer at low heat for two hours until meat almost falls to pieces in the gravy. Stir occasionally. Serve this Texas style swiss steak with rice and a good salad.

REED BIRDS

Vivian Turnball of Battleground, Washington suggests that these reed birds or bobolinks be stuffed with oysters.

Pick and draw—clean and pluck feathers—reed birds very carefully; salt and pepper and dredge them with flour. Roast 10-15 minutes at high heat, in a pan on top of the stove or in a hot oven. Serve on toast with butter and more pepper, if desired. If desired, stuff with an oyster dipped in butter and coated with bread crumbs before roasting. If oysters are small and birds are big, use more than one. (Just one oyster was probably considered a treat.)

ROAST VENISON

LaNelle E. Davis of Broken Bow, Oklahoma, uses this recipe for venison, like her grandmother did before her.

Venison
Vinegar to wash venison plus ½ c. to roast venison
1 clove garlic minced
1 onion chopped

Wash meat in vinegar and water to remove odor. In a washed tin can, put garlic, onion, vinegar, and one cup of water. Bring to boil on stove; when you smell the vinegar, pour it on top of the meat. Roast in oven at 325°, until done and tender, about 2 to 3 hours, to suit taste for rare, medium or well done meat.

WILD TURKEY (FROM JOHN NORWOOD)

So many of these birds were killed for food that they almost became extinct. But now they are coming back.

Use your favorite tame turkey stuffing. Make it a bit moister and add a couple tablespoons of cooking oil, butter, or bacon grease. After stuffing both cavities, secure with skewers and string and truss the wings and legs close to the body with string. Rub well with fat. Roast in a 325° oven allowing about 22-25 minutes per pound. If breast is browning too fast cover with foil or rind from a slab of bacon. Baste often with fat mixed with dry white wine. After removing the bird from the oven skim off most of the fat from drippings. Stir in a little flour with milk or water. Add a pinch of seasoning to taste. Bring to a heat that will make a medium thick gravy.

ROASTED WILD TURKEY WITH HERBED CORN BREAD STUFFING

This recipe which appeared in "Pioneers Talked Turkey" (November, 1984 *True West*), can be adapted to the domesticated turkey for your Thanksgiving dinner:

1 dressed turkey about 12 lbs. fresh or frozen with giblets	⅓ c. fresh herbs consisting of ¼ c. sage or 2 T. dried herbs
one pan of corn bread	pepper to taste
¾ to 1 lb. cornbread	½ c. all-purpose flour

Simmer giblets in saucepan in 3 cups water. After 10 minutes remove liver; continue simmering the rest for about an hour; set aside to cool.

Break corn bread fine in a bowl. Add enough water to moisten; squeeze bread. Cut salt pork into thin slices. Set aside several slices and chop the rest almost fine. Chop liver fine. Crush sage and other herbs. Stir herbs into bread with pepper.

Preheat oven to 325°. Rinse bird and pat dry. Pack stuffing loosely in cavity and crop flap.

Grease the pan and bird with salt pork slices. Shake coating of flour over the turkey. Slip two slices of pork under the roast and place two slices on the breast. Place in the oven.

After 1 hour pour 1 cup water over the turkey and dust it again with flour. After 2 hours raise the temperature to 350° and baste well with pan liquid. Continue to baste every 20 minutes, adding water as needed.

Meanwhile remove the giblets from the broth. Set aside. Blend 2 tablespoons flour with enough broth. Gradually blend the paste into the remaining broth.

At 3 hours begin testing the turkey for doneness. An old cookbook says "A sure test is the readiness of the joints to separate from the body." If you can't do this, roast up to one-half hour longer.

Remove the turkey to a warm platter. Skim any clear fat from pan. Stir broth into pan and heat until the liquid thickens gravy to taste. Season.

FRIED TROUT

8-oz. trout, cleaned,
  with heads and tails
freshly ground pepper
1 heaping T. your choice of herbs
¼ c. cornmeal

¼ c. flour
1 T. butter and
  6 T. oil or bacon grease
lemon, cut in wedges

Wash trout and pat dry. Sprinkle cavities and skins of fish evenly with pepper and herbs. Spread the cornmeal and flour mixture on wax paper.

In a large skillet, melt the butter and oil over high heat. When the foam subsides, roll each trout in the meal and flour and place fish in the skillet. Fry the trout for 5 minutes, then turn over carefully with a spatula. Continue to fry until the trout are crisp and golden brown. Serve with lemon.

POACHED TROUT OR SALMON

Use a poaching basket or make one from clean rabbit netting wire or use a steamer. Place gutted fish in the basket placed on a rack just above boiling water in a large pan and cover. Cook until fish is done, and is easily flaked. The fish can also be cooked covered in a moderate oven. Let cool awhile, then carefully remove the fish from the basket. Serve with lemon.

Herbed Fish—trout and salmon

INDIAN SALMON

The Indians of the Northwest Coast prepared for the year's first salmon run guided by their religious beliefs. The ceremonial feast known as the Potlatch left the host's cupboard bare, but in turn he would partake of the generosity of another host. The menu for the feast included many different courses of salmon and usually ended with squaw candy, salmon that had been salted, smoked and dried in strips. Squaw candy can be as chewy as a licorice stick, if not as tasty.

To cook salmon the Indian way, clean and flatten it, and douse it with seal oil or any other oil. Insert between two upright poles, braced with splints. The poles should be slanted toward or away from the open fire to regulate the speed of cooking. Cook till done. Salmon can be cooked in the oven but it won't be Indian salmon.

TROUT WITH MINT

Mix a good supply of mint, 1 cup fresh mint leaves, with one tablespoon of oil, mashing to a pulp. Put a spoonful or so inside each trout. Close the cavity and wrap with bacon, holding in place with toothpicks. Lay the trout on your grill, and cook basting with more of the mint and oil mixture. When fish flakes when prodded with a fork it is done. Don't overcook; it should take about ten minutes.

MONA BASIN STUFFED TROUT

Like the Indians of the Northwest, the Basques in California's Mona Basin ate a lot of fish. This recipe originated with Basque sheepherders.

4 cloves finely minced garlic
½ c. bread crumbs
½ tsp. thyme
½ tsp. basil
½ tsp. sugar

½ c. parsley
¼ c. olive oil
4 cleaned trout about ½ lb. each
4 thin slices of serrano or
   other smoked ham

Combine all ingredients but ham and trout. Add pepper to taste; the ham is salty enough. Stuff each trout with a slice of ham and enough of the crumb mixture to fill the body cavity. Close with a skewer if necessary.

Put above ¼ cup olive oil in a heavy cast iron or earthenware dish; add fish and put into oven at 350° until done, about 15 to 20 minutes.

Sauce

¼ butter
¼ c. olive oil
1-3 cloves garlic to taste,
   finely minced

1 tsp. paprika
1 T. fresh minced or
½ tsp. dried basil
½ c. cream sherry

While fish are in the oven, heat butter and oil in a heavy pan on stove top. Add remaining ingredients. Cook over a high flame stirring constantly, until liquid is somewhat thickened. When the fish are done, cover with sauce and garnish with watercress and twists of lemon.

FRIZZLED BEEF, RECIPE 1

Frizzled beef is one of those forgotten frontier foods (mentioned in the four-part series in *True West*, "Forgotten Frontier Foods"). Great-grandpa enjoyed a sizzling dish of frizzled jerky for his midday meal.

3 oz. pkg. dried beef, cut in thin strips
¼ c. butter, plus 1 T.
¼ c. flour
2 c. milk

Fry beef in 1 T. butter till it frizzles in the skillet. In a pan melt butter and add flour and blend. Add milk and stir till sauce is smooth and thickened. Serve the beef and sauce separately or mix together. (If too salty, boil meat before frying.)

FRIZZLED BEEF, RECIPE 2

From Vivian Turnball of Battleground, Washington, comes this campfire variation of frizzled beef. (You can cook it on the stove, too.)

¼ to ½ lb. smoked or dried beef
1 oz. sweet butter or grease
3 eggs
buttered toast or biscuits

Shave off very thin slices of smoked or dried beef; put them in a frying pan, and cover with cold water. Set it on the fire and cook over slow heat. Allow it to swell, then drain off the water and set aside the beef.

Melt an ounce of sweet butter or grease in the pan, then add the beef. When it begins to turn up, add the eggs and stir until they are cooked. Add pepper and serve over buttered toast or biscuits. The toast can also be spread with bacon grease.

Frizzled Beef with biscuits and pickles

FRIED MEAT CAKES OR PIONEER HAMBURGERS

1 lb. lean raw meat	1-2 eggs
seasonings	½-1 c. breadcrumbs
1 onion	drippings

Chop the meat, as you would for sausage; season with salt, pepper, and onion, and shape into flat cakes. Dip the cakes in egg and breadcrumbs and fry in drippings. Drain on a strainer. Have ready a dish of creamy mashed potatoes.

SPICY CHOCOLATE STUFFING

Chocolate wasn't only for desserts. The Southwest Indians enhanced their venison with a sauce seasoned with chocolate. It was similar to the mole served with turkey in the Southwest today. The following recipe is a cross between a mole and piccadillo.

1 lb. ground beef, browned	1 c. beef consomme
2 c. white raisins	Use a variety that is not salty.
1 to 2 oz. unsweetened chocolate, melted	1 tsp. ground cinnamon
	1 tsp. ground coriander
1 c. roasted pinons— no substitutes if you want to be authentic	½ tsp. ground cloves
	½ c. red wine

Combine all ingredients except wine; simmer until thick, stirring constantly. Add wine and bring to boil. Set aside to cool if to be used as a stuffing. Otherwise, serve as the main course, with southwestern bread and an avocado salad with fruit.

BAKED HASH

From the pages of an old cookbook belonging to Eunice Christian of Yellville, Arkansas comes this recipe for baked hash.

Her mother cut recipes from newspapers and pasted them in this book. When her mother died in 1912, she left her daughter some old-fashioned recipes.

2 c. chopped, cooked meat	1 clove of garlic, minced
2. c. raw potatoes, diced	salt and pepper to taste
¼ c. melted butter	1 T. of favorite herb (optional)
½ minced onion	
1 c. bread crumbs	sprinkle of paprika
2 egg yolks	
1¼ c. meat stock	

Combine meat, potatoes, butter (save one tablespoon), onions, garlic, ⅓ cup bread crumbs, egg yolks, stock and seasoning. Add the remaining ⅔ cup bread crumbs as a topping and drizzle with the rest of the butter. Sprinkle with paprika. Bake for one hour at 350°.

VEAL LOAF

Remember the cracker barrel? Some of those crackers from the country store were used to make this easy meat loaf recipe from Jean Peterson of Correctionville, Iowa.

3 lb. chopped veal
¼ lb. salt pork chopped fine
1 c. rolled crackers
2 eggs
1 tsp. pepper
dash of pepper

Make these ingredients into a loaf and bake two hours.

MOUNTAIN DIP STEAK OF LEAN

William Newton of Alabama prefers this to today's bacon. Call it fat back, salt pork, sow belly, or side meat, but enjoy the taste of sugar cured ham or Canadian bacon.

½ lb. side meat,
  sliced the way you like it
1 T. sorghum syrup

Fill a large frying pan with water; let it come to a boil. Then add one tablespoon of syrup; mix well. Remove from heat. Dip the meat and let it drip. Then fry at medium heat in another pan.

SAUSAGES IN SAVORY GRAVY

The following recipe is a favorite California ranch dish at breakfast time.

2 link sausages per person,
  with the skins pricked
  to prevent bursting
¼ c. cream sherry
1 sliced onion
3 minced cloves of garlic
1 T. flour
1 c. stock
½ c. mushrooms, optional
¼ c. fresh parsley
  or 1 T. dried parsley
¼ tsp. chili powder
freshly ground pepper

Saute sausages in pan until nicely browned. Remove from the pan and keep warm. Add inexpensive (California) cream sherry to pan juices and heat until bubbling. Add onion and garlic; saute until done and remove from pan. Put with the sausages to keep warm.

Add the flour to the pan. Stirring constantly over a high heat, cook until browned. Gradually add the stock, stirring constantly until resulting gravy is the consistency you wish. (There should be about 1 cup liquid for each tablespoon of flour in the mixture.) Continue cooking over low heat for another 15 to 20 minutes, stirring frequently. If you wish, add some sliced mushrooms and a bit of parsley. Add the chili powder and pepper to taste.

Put the sausages and onions in a heated serving dish and pour the savory heated gravy over them. Sprinkle with chopped greens from spring onion, if desired. Serve hot with boiled potatoes or hash browns.

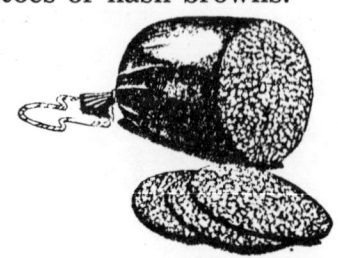

HOLIDAY GOOSE

Prepare one young goose, about 8 to 12 pounds, as you would a turkey. Then prick the fatty skin. Fill the cavity with dressing such as apple, prune or chestnut, or with cut onion, garlic or leeks sprinkled with sage and marjoram.

Preheat oven to 450°. While waiting, rub herbs over goose: parsley, sage, rosemary and thyme. Place goose on rack in uncovered pan; allow about 25 minutes per pound. Reduce heat to 350° after goose is in oven. Remove excess fat; keep for cooking. A half hour before goose is done, turn it over once to insure a crisp skin. After your goose is cooked, decorate with cranberry garland.

Holiday Goose with trimmings

ONION STUFFING (Suggested for Goose)

Goose broth
8 c. bread or corn bread or a mixture, crumbled
2 c. chopped onion
¼ c. butter
1 egg
1 T. powdered sage or a small handful of crumbled leaves
minced giblets (optional)

Make a broth by boiling in advance the goose neck with the liver, heart, gizzard. Cook the onion in the butter until the onion starts to wilt and brown slightly. Mix into the bread, the onions, egg, sage, and enough broth to moisten the stuffing. Use this stuffing to fill the cavities of the goose.

SQUATUM BAKED HAM

"Squatum" means picnic. Take along some watercress and some pickled crabapples to garnish your picnic ham.

To make squatum, bake a ham in the normal fashion. Baste it frequently with cider mixed with an equal amount of pan juices. When done, let cool and remove the skin and most of the fat. Using the handle of a large wooden spoon, make a hole in all the way through the center of the ham. Start in the centerfront, without tearing sides, and chisel out a space in which to insert the stuffing. Don't go through the other end. Only one of four sides should be opened.

Mix well together:
1 c. cream cheese
1 c. cheddar cheese, grated
¼ c. crumbled blue cheese
½ c. parsley, finely minced
1 onion, finely minced
¼ c. brown sugar
½ c. port wine

Chill until firm. Pack into the center of the ham and chill thoroughly. To serve, slice and arrange on a platter.

MAMMY'S STUFFED SQUATUM CRABS

From a slave cabin in Georgia to elegant mansions in San Fransico, Mary Ellen Pleasants, affectionately known as Mammy, worked to achieve celebrity status as a chef. Here is her recipe for picnic crabs:

4 crabs, cleaned
1 c. mayonnaise
2 T. mild chili sauce
1 onion, minced
2 green onions,
  chopped into pieces
2 cloves garlic, finely minced
1 tsp. Dijon-type mustard
2 hard-boiled eggs, diced
½ tsp. dill weed
a touch of sugar
  and a dash of salt
lettuce and garnishes

Remove the legs from the crabs. Remove the meat from the bodies. Save the top shells. Flake the meat and mix with all the other ingredients, except lettuce.

For each serving, line a plate with crisp greens. Put a portion of the crab mixture in the center. Cover with one of the top shells. Arrange the legs around the shell to resemble the whole crab. Garnish with tomato wedges, black olives, and lemon slices.

SAUERKRAUT STUFFING

Although any stuffing recipe that suits your fancy can suit your pig, we include one for sauerkraut.

5 c. bread crumbled
4 c. sauerkraut, drained, but save
  liquid for stuffing
3 T. brown sugar
2 garlic cloves, minced
1 large onion chopped
2 tart apples, peeled, cored
  and chopped
½ c. dried currants
1 c. chestnuts, chopped
½ tsp. ground marjoram

Combine all ingredients and add enough liquid to moisten to your taste in stuffing.

SUCKLING PIG

1-12 lb. suckling pig
2½ qts. of dressing
butter and garlic mix
  (about ¼ c. butter and 1 clove
    garlic minced.)
¼ c. flour
1 apple
2 cranberries or raisins

Preferably, the butcher will draw, scrape and clean the pig for you. The dressed pig should weigh about 12 pounds.

Prepare 2½ quarts of dressing. Stuff the opening with the dressing and then sew up the pig. Put a block of wood in its mouth to hold it open. Skewer the legs into position, pulling the forelegs forward and bending the hind legs into a crouching stance. Rub the pig with butter and garlic. Dredge with flour. Cover the ears and tail with foil.

Place in a pan in 450° oven for 15 minutes. Reduce heat to 325° and roast, allowing 30 minutes per pound. Baste every hour with the pan juices and, if needed, stock. When the pig is tender, remove the foil. Place the pig on a platter and remove wood from the mouth and replace it with an apple. Place cranberries or raisins in the eyes. Enjoy your holiday dinner!

CHICKEN PIES

Pot pies on the prairie for Sunday dinner or special picnics were always memorable. Paul Brunner's favorite was made with his Montana chickens. These are good for a Fourth of July picnic.

9 c. chopped chicken
6 c. chopped potatoes
½ c. chopped onions
3 c. chopped celery
9 c. chopped carrots
2 c. whole peas
1 c. flour
4 c. broth from chicken and
  veggies or 2 c. milk and
  2 of broth
pie dough, enough for 4 single
  crust or 2 double crust pies

If using a fresh chicken, boil it and take the meat off the bone; chop or grind coarsely. Boil all the vegetables together. Take the vegetable water and chicken broth to make gravy.

Melt the butter. Add the flour and stir till smooth. Then add the liquid. Cook until thick.

Put the chicken and vegetables in your casserole, pie pans, or individual tart tins. You may optionally sprinkle with some herbs and pepper.

Roll out the pastry to fit the top or tops of your pie(s). Remove a circle of dough from the center, and if you have one, insert a china pie bird. Otherwise make a design in the crust. Bake at 350° for 30 to 45 minutes. (You may freeze the pies without cooking.)

The pie is good at different temperatures.

SUNDAY CHICKEN PIES

2 chickens, disjointed, with giblets
2 large onions, minced
flour for coating
fat for browning
2 teeth garlic, minced
2 or 3 carrots, cut in bite-size chunks
1 c. peas
1 c. green beans
1 c. green beans
1 c. corn, cut from the cob
2 or 3 potatoes, cut in bite-size chunks
½ c. minced parsley
1 tsp. mixed herbs
additional gravy, if needed
favorite pie crust

Put giblets, backs and necks in water to cover and cook until meat is tender, about 2 hours. Shake chicken pieces in flour and saute in hot fat until browned. Place in bottom of deep, ovenproof dish.

Sprinkle the rest of the ingredients over the chicken. Mix 1 tablespoon flour and 1 tablespoon butter and stir into stock from the giblets. Pour over chicken and vegetables. Cover all with your favorite pie crust. Crimp and paint with a beaten egg. Put in oven at 325° and bake for about 1½-2 hours.

CORNISH PASTIES

Essentially a pastie is a Mulligan stew in a crust. They were popular at the noon lunch, but at home often served as a morning or evening meal. Pasties were brought to the West by the Cornish. They were a noon meal in themselves for the hard-working miners. John Norwood of Arvada, Colorado, in his book of early-day dishes that moved from the Atlantic to the Pacific during the great Westerning, mentions that pasties were popular on the trail and in the mines.

3 c. unsifted flour
1¼ c. shortening
¾ c. very cold water
5 or 6 medium potatoes— Red McClures, best
3 medium size, strong onions, peeled
2 lb. meat, diced or thinly sliced
sage, salt, pepper to your taste

Measure and mix flour (and salt). Cut in shortening with a couple of knives like making pie crust. Add water and mix gently using knives, fork, or a pastry blender. Work enough for dough to stick together and form into a roll. Cut into 3 pieces.

Roll each piece of dough thin and somewhat oblong. On each rolled out piece of dough slice the potatoes, and onions, and meat in layers and mix them. Put on the dough at the same time.

Wet the top edges of the oblong of dough, bring up and squeeze and crimp together so that the meat and vegetables are sealed in. Bake at 350° to 375° until done, about one hour. For a better looking pastie, brush with canned milk about halfway through the cooking.

You can bake these in a Dutch oven covered or an open pan. If covered, the dough will be like a dumpling. Accompany with beer, fried chicken, homemade bread and potato salad.

BLACKBIRD PIE

Instead of four and twenty blackbirds baked within a pie, we have four and eight. Waldo Olson's parents found this recipe in a cookbook accompanying their Home Comfort Range when they set up housekeeping in Nebraska at the turn of the century.

12 blackbirds or
 any other small game birds
pepper to taste
¼ c. parsley
1 c. onion, chopped
3 cloves, whole
1 c. salt pork

2 c. potatoes, sliced
2 T. flour, browned
2 T. butter
a pastry crust

Clean the birds. Split each in half. Place in stew pan with water to cover. Bring to boil, skimming off scum or impurities. Add sprinkling of pepper, parsley, onion, and cloves; then add salt pork and boil until meat is tender about an hour. During the last half hour of cooking, add potatoes. Remove the mixture from the broth.

Thicken broth with flour and boil for a few minutes. Add one tablespoon of the butter, mix and remove from fire. Grease baking dish with the other tablespoon of butter and put in alternate layers of birds and potatoes, moistening each layer with broth. Cover with pastry crust. Slit crust in several places. Bake for 15 minutes at 425°, then bake another 25 minutes at 375° or until browned.

SOLE A LA MARGUERY A LA DIAMOND JIM BRADY
(Diamond Jim Brady made a fortune selling railroad supplies)

2 c. water
½ c. carrots, sliced
½ c. leeks or onions, chopped
10 whole peppercorns
3 sprigs parsley
1 bay leaf
½ tsp. dried thyme, crushed or
 1½ tsp. fresh
1 lb. fresh or frozen
 sole fillets, thawed

1 lb. fresh or frozen haddock
 or other white fish
½ lb. fresh or frozen shrimp
1 c. shucked oyster, fresh or
 same amount frozen or canned
½ c. butter
¼ c. dry white wine
4 slightly beaten egg yolks

In a saucepan combine water, carrots, leeks, peppercorns, parsley, bay, and thyme; bring to boiling. Add sole and haddock. Reduce heat and cook about 5 minutes.

Strain, reserving stock. Arrange sole and haddock in buttered rectangular dish; top with 1 c. of fish stock. Arrange shrimp and oysters atop fish. Cover; bake at 325° till fish flakes easily when tested with a fork, about 15 minutes. Carefully lift fillets, oysters, and shrimp to hot oven-proof platter. Reserve juices, keep the fish and seafood hot. Meanwhile, boil 1 c. of reserved stock till reduced to ¼ c.; place in top of double boiler. Add butter and wine. Place over hot water; cook and stir just till butter melts. Add egg yolks; cook and stir till thickened. Pour over fish, oysters, and shrimp broil 4 inches from heat till lightly browned, 2-3 minutes.

ROCKY MOUNTAIN OYSTERS

After branding and castrating the calves, cattle ranchers often hold a big feed of the "oysters."

Skin and wash the testicles. Dip them in egg and flour or an egg-flour batter; season and fry in bacon drippings, lard or oil until browned and tender. Accompany with beer, fried chicken, homemade bread and potato salad.

To prepare your "oysters" cowboy style, roast them over the coals of a hot fire until these delicacies pop open.

For about a pound of "oysters" use one of the following recipes:

2 eggs   1 c. flour

or:

2 eggs   ½ c. milk
1 c. flour   1 c. bacon drippings

Vary proportions to suit amount of "oysters."

CALF'S HEAD

On a roundup the cowhands generally killed a ten or eleven-month-old suckling calf. It was usually butchered late in the evening. John W. Moore, of El Paso, Texas, gives directions for cooking the head.

Dig a hole about two feet deep, and in it build a fire of hardwood, mesquite, or oak. Put some rocks on top of the wood and let the fire burn down to coals.

Without cleaning or washing it, wrap the calf's head in wet gunny sacks "good and tight." Remove some of the coals and rocks. Put the head in the hole and cover it with about two inches of dirt. Build a fire on top of the dirt with mesquite wood. Let it cook all night for six or more hours.

Remove the calf's head from the hole, and it will be ready to eat. The hide will pull away from the flesh. "You will find the meat, the brains, and the tongue very fine eating," says John, who has seen the cowhands fight over the eyeballs.

KLOOK—BLOOD MEATBALLS

Unsavory and savory at the same time is this recipe from Walt Thayer who received the recipe from a German immigrant in Idaho. It is actually an old Norwegian dish.

Catch a large dishpan of fresh blood from a cow or pig when butchering. Keep stirring it until it separates and the albumin and white corpuscles cling together; throw that part away. Mix the pure red blood with rye flour and season it with salt and pepper. Roll the mixture into balls, like tennis balls, and put a chunk of fat or lard in the center of each. Boil them and serve hot. You can dice them and serve with butter and raw onions.

EATING WHAT
COMES NATURALLY

Herbs and spices, including flowers, greens, and weeds, were used to flavor drinks and food. Indians taught white settlers to eat many roots, shoots, stalks, and seeds. Settlers foraged for greens such as pokeweed, plantain, and lamb's quarters. Cattail to Indians and settlers alike was a seasoning and all purpose herb. The tender young shoots were good steamed and served as greens; the pollen went into baked goods.

Dock, a heavy seeder, was one of the most common foods among Indians. If not cooked as a vegetable, it was a good source of flour or meal. The Indians didn't need salt when they had natural foods and seasonings like peppergrass, from the mustard family, and coltsfoot, a tobacco substitute.

Indians smoked herbs in modest quantities considered beneficial. One of the healthiest herbs was goldenrod. Brewed into tea, it was flavorful and nutritious. Herbs for teas were often gathered in threes. Drinking tea probably more than smoking pipes, kept Indians healthy.

Lewis and Clark found the Northwest Indians digging for arrowhead, or wapatoo. The squaws dug the tubers with their toes, steamed them in pits, and dried them for the winter. The women pounded the onion-shaped bulb of the camass, or quamash, into a type of bread. With its potato-like taste, the camass was also steamed in pits.

The settlers quickly grew fond of the native fruits and berries. Some foods now considered gourmet were staples among the Indians, particularly wild rice and pinenuts.

The earliest settlers brought herb seeds from Europe. Bee balm and lemon balm provided cures when there were no corner drugstores. Bee balm was used as a sleeping aid and cure for colds. It was also a great insect repellent. Lemon balm provided a cure for sores if applied as a poultice or insect repellent. Many believed that it increased the flow of milk in cows and insured longevity in humans. Penny-royal was the best pest repellent in the summer, and in the winter it provided the best relief from colds. Catnip was harvested for tea to be drunk when one was out of sorts. Many on the great westering movement drank mint tea to relieve bodily distress. Many herbs grew wild in the woods; others were planted in the kitchen garden.

One description of an early herb garden included cabbages, parsnips, carrots, dill, salad, sorrel, radishes, cress, leeks, rosemary, lavender, laurel, artichokes, and asparagus. The artichokes were most likely to be Jerusalem artichokes and the term salad meant different greens. Sorrel not only added a lemony zest to soups and salads but also tenderized meat and removed spots from clothes.

Parsley, sage, rosemary, and thyme added flavor to soup that was frozen and stored in the shed or in the snow. Sage was used in mock duck and stuffings and to darken Great-grandma's greying hair. If Great-grandma was a blonde, she might color her hair with chamomille tea. Chamomille also made a good tea to induce sleep and ease menstrual cramps.

Flowers, too, were used to flavor. Marigold and chrysanthemum blossoms were put in salads and batter-dipped for good eating. Clover was a tasty, healthful additive. Tansy perked up egg dishes and flavored custard in place of vanilla. Some pioneers, however, were wary of tansy because of suspected abortive properties.

Dandelions were welcome on the homestead. The leaves were eaten in salads or cooked dishes; the flowers were used to make wine. Finally, the roots were ground for coffee.

Pioneers in the West had to be resourceful just to survive. It took even more ingenuity to add a little spice to their lives.

CHAPTER 6
Leaves, Roots and Grains
Vegetables

DANDELION FRITTERS (CORNMEAL HUSH PUPPIES)

1 c. cornmeal
2 T. flour
½ tsp. soda
1 egg, beaten
¾ c. buttermilk
3 T. onion, finely chopped
½ c. dandelion greens, chopped
fat, oil or lard
  (chicken grease is good)

In a large bowl stir together cornmeal, flour, and soda. In a small bowl stir together the egg, buttermilk, onion, and chopped greens. Stir the liquid ingredients into the cornmeal mixture, just till the dry ingredients are moistened.

In a large skillet melt enough fat to fry the fritters. Fat should be ½ inch deep in skillet. Drop the batter by tablespoonful into the hot fat, spreading it slightly to make a patty. Fry till golden, 2-3 minutes, turning once. Drain and serve.

WILD ONIONS

These grow near creek banks and are much smaller than onions grown in your garden. Clean them and boil in water until tender. Then they may be put in a skillet with some cooking oil and eggs. Stir until the eggs are cooked. Serve hot.

POKESALAD

The parents of Ardis Shilton of Flat, Texas, always looked for the first polk plants or pokeweed, in the spring. The plants grew in scattered areas over their place.

greens
water, salted or unsalted
onions, optional
bacon grease

Take off any tough stems and seeds. Cover with water. Cook greens until tender; then drain and rinse them one time. At this point, cook chopped onions in the grease if desired. Cover the bottom of a pan or skillet with bacon grease. Add the greens and simmer ten minutes.

GRANNY'S SPECIAL

Bill Newton of Elmore, Alabama, likes foraging for greens, and cattails. His granny's granny gave him many recipes. Spinach or other greens can be substituted for pokesalad.

1 lb. ground meat
2 onions, chopped
2 c. pokesalad, chopped
2 eggs, beaten

Cook meat and onions together until done. Drain off the washed pokesalad. Cook meat, onions, and greens together for about 10 minutes; add eggs last. Cook until eggs are done. Serve hot.

CATTAIL BUD PILAF

The Indians taught the pioneers to use cattails from the marshes and ponds for food and other products.

2 c. fresh, green cattail buds, scraped from spikes
¼ c. onions, chopped
¼ c. vegetable oil or butter
1 egg, beaten
2 c. rice or bulgur wheat, cooked
¼ c. nutmeats or sunflower kernels

In large, heavy fry pan saute the onions in oil or butter to prevent sticking. Fry the egg in the form of a large thin pancake. When egg is dry and slightly browned, turn out onto cutting board. Slice into thin slivers.

Add the rice or bulgur to the cattail mixture and combine. Gently add the egg strips and heat through. Add the nutmeats or sunflower kernels and season to taste.

WILD GREENS

Pick young and wash. Dandelions, poke, dock, wild lettuce, wild mustard, lambs-quarters, tops of wild beets, etc. all produce tasty greens. Place in a saucepan and cover with water. Boil about 15 to 20 minutes. Drain well. You can eat them boiled or you can fry them in grease about 15 minutes.

Spring greens team up with onions, bacon, etc.

FRIED HUCKLEBERRIES OR BLUEBERRIES

Huckleberries resemble blueberries. Use one or the other or combine.

Mix one quart of fresh huckleberries with one cup of sugar. Fry in a skillet containing ⅔ cup of shortening for about ten minutes. Serve hot with biscuits.

INDIAN MUSHROOMS

Soak mushrooms overnight in salt water. Season cleaned mushrooms and roll in flour. Fry in hot grease until brown. Serve hot.

WILD RICE WITH MUSHROOMS AND HICKORY NUTS

You can also try the recipe with pinenuts. Or, instead of all wild rice, try using some brown rice.

5 T. butter, divided	½ c. hickory nuts, chopped in small pieces
2 T. onions	
1 c. wild rice	½ lb. fresh mushrooms, sliced ½ inch thick
2 c. stock or water	

Preheat oven to 350°. In a heavy 2 quart casserole with a lid, melt 2 tablespoons of the butter over moderate heat. Add the onions; cook for about 5 minutes, stirring.

Add the rice and stir until the grains are coated. Then pour in stock and stir until the mixture comes to a boil.

Scatter 2 T. of butter bits on top. Cover the casserole. Bake in the middle of the oven and let the rice rest at room temperature for 15 minutes, uncovered.

Meanwhile melt one tablespoon of butter in a heavy 10-inch skillet and brown the nuts for a minute or two, stirring evenly. With a slotted spoon remove the nuts and drain them on paper towels.

Add mushrooms and cook for 10 to 15 minutes, stirring occasionally, until all the moisture they give off has evaporated. Season.

To serve, combine the rice and mushrooms in a bowl and toss them together. Scatter the nuts on top and serve.

CORN ON THE COB

Davilla Bright, of Norman, Oklahoma, has some words on its proper cooking.

Fresh, tender corn, shucked, and silked (silks removed) reaches its best stage of tenderness if boiled only five minutes. A dash of sugar in the water adds to the flavor of the corn. Longer boiling produces hard, tough, darkened kernels of corn. Five minutes of boiling makes it just right.

CREAMED CORN

A can of corn from the store with some special cooking at home could make Mrs. Bright's company corn. The secret is mostly in having the bacon drippings steaming hot when you empty the can of corn into that skillet. Stir to keep from scorching. Then add seasonings to taste, a pinch of sugar and 1 tablespoon of flour mixed in a cup of milk, and stir into the cooking corn. Cook until done about 5 minutes.

WAGON TRAIL CORN

Corn, grits and water make a soup to eat on or off the trail. Lenora Taylor of Oklahoma cooked this soup.

Parch corn in hot ashes until brown. Sift ashes out of corn and beat until a grit stage is reached. Sift meal until nothing but the grits are left. Add grits to hot water to make a soup to suit your taste.

PARCHED CORN

For one cup of parched corn you will need 1 ear of dried field corn or 1 cup of dried sweet corn. If you are using field corn, shell it and remove the chaff by tossing handfuls back and forth. Heat 2 T. of butter in a skillet over high heat. Cover the pan with kernels of corn, reduce heat slightly, and stir constantly as the kernels brown, puff up, and crackle. Cook 3 to 5 minutes. Remove the pan from the heat, season to taste and serve.

POPCORN FOR DINNER

My great-grandmother remembered eating popcorn as cereal for dinner. When the cupboard was bare, it was one of the few foods available. For tradition's sake, the family would have Sunday night popcorn suppers even when the lean years were over.

T. D. Church, of Bellvue, Washington, remembers his grandfather's tales about early day puffed cereal. He grew a little popcorn patch over 120 years ago. He poured thick cream over a bowl of popcorn and added a sprinkling of sugar.

MEAT STRETCHER

When money was short or when unexpected company knocked on the door, this meat and rice dish was a treat, especially with different seasonings. Mrs. MaryAnne McDonald of Saskatchewan can vouch for that.

2 T. bacon fat
1 onion
1 c. rice, non-instant
2 c. canned tomatoes, drained, or fresh
2 c. cold leftover meat
2 c. hot water
herbs and spices
1 dash of cayenne pepper
1 tsp. salt, optional

Put the fat in the frying pan and cut in the onion; fry to delicate brown in the hot fat, but do not let it burn. Next add the tomatoes, meat, and 2 cups of hot water. Cover and cook till the rice is done. Add more water if needed, but the dish should not be watery when done. Season with cayenne, curry powder, and whatever else you like.

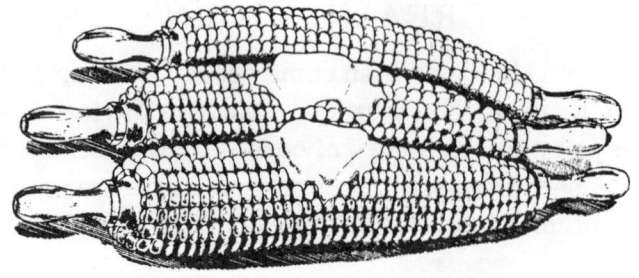

HOMINY SCRAPPLE

Hominy is a uniquely American food; so is scrapple. The hominy in this recipe substitutes for the pork usually in scrapple. Eloise Rushing, of Whitesboro, Texas contributed this recipe.

1 can hominy
1 onion, cut in small pieces
1 heaping T. lard
1 dash cayenne pepper
1 tsp. salt, optional

Grind hominy in food chopper. Set aside. Fry onions in lard. Add tomatoes and seasonings; cook 15-20 minutes. Add hominy and cook about 5 minutes more.

ONION PIE

This pie with no upper crust is of German origin. James Fury, who operates a mail order recipe service in Texas, specializes in onion pie. In Germany "Zwiebelkuchen" is a favorite in the fall as accompaniment to the "New Wine." This wine, not fully matured, is somewhere between grape juice and wine. And whether you know it or not, the Germans are the largest ethnic group in Texas, contributing their share to "the biggest little kitchen in the West."

6 onions, sliced
butter and lard for frying
¾ c. milk plus a few spoons more
½ c. cream
1 egg, beaten
1 T. flour
½ tsp. salt, optional
¼ tsp. pepper
1 pie crust

Fry the onions in a skillet with butter and lard. When they are soft add the milk and the cream and the egg. Thicken this with the flour and seasoning mixed smooth in a few spoons of cold milk.

Have ready a crust in 1 9-inch pie plate. Fill with onion mixture and bake at 350° for 35-45 minutes, till the filling is set and browned.

GREEN CORN OYSTERS

Real oysters were often a treat in the old West, whether fresh or tinned. Oysters came in forms other than the bivalve mollusk, though, including Rocky Mountain oysters, and this recipe for vegetable oysters comes from Walt Thayer.

1 pint young green corn, grated
1 egg, well beaten
1 c. flour
2 to 3 T. butter
salt and pepper to taste
fat for frying

In a dish containing the corn and egg, mix the flour, butter and seasonings to make a batter. Drop one tablespoon of batter into deep fat to make each oyster. Fry the oysters until they are light brown. Serve buttered.

PEA SAUSAGE

When meat was scarce these black-eyed pea sausages were eaten at any meal—mornings with eggs and biscuits and nights with vegetables. California's La Verne E. Ray, likes to top these off with delicious vinegar pie (Chapter 9) for dessert.

2 c. black-eyed peas,
  seasoned and cooked, or canned
black pepper, sage,
  and salt to taste
½ c. flour
¼ c. bacon fat,
  oil or grease

Drain black-eyed peas. Mash with fork; season to taste. Add just enough flour to make it all stick together. Shape into patties and fry in hot oil or grease until brown.

CALIFORNIA PICNIC SALAD

6 large potatoes, peeled
  and boiled until tender
  but not mushy
2 purple onions
  cut into thin rings
2 stalks of celery
1 c. fresh or frozen peas
¼ c. parsley, finely minced
½ c. each red and green bell
  pepper, cut into thin slices
2 chicken breasts,
  steamed until done
  and cut into strips
1 can black pitted olives

DRESSING

1½ c. mayonnaise
4 c. country-style chili sauce
4 cloves garlic, finely minced
1 tsp. dill weed
1 T. Dijon mustard

Drain and dice potatoes. Add all next seven ingredients and set aside. Combine dressing ingredients and blend well. Spoon dressing over salad and toss lightly until well-mixed. Line a serving dish with crisp lettuce and pile the salad into the lettuce center. Garnish with tomato slices and more black olives.

COWBOY SALAD

According to Dr. B. F. Ederer of Bonita, California, spicy cowboy salad accompanied the wild pig at a Gila Bend javelina barbecue. All of this exceptionally good "chow" was wetted down with copious quantities of cowboy coffee.

large can tomatoes, about
  2 pounds, drained, and cut up
1 can diced chilies
  (Add what amounts chilies
  and pickles please you.)
1 large onion, diced
diced dill pickles
seasonings to taste
vinegar and oil to taste with
  a dash of mustard

Combine the ingredients in the order given; then toss all together.

SKILLET POTATOES WITH ONIONS

Bill Dunn, of Alexandria, Louisiana, submitted the Old West Recipe for Spring, 1984.

6 slices bacon,
  about ¼ inch thick
1 large Irish potato,
  cut into ¼ inch slices
1 bunch (about 6) fresh
  green onions, cleaned and
  cut into 1-inch lengths
  or 3 onions with
  a handful of chives

In a hot skillet (preferably cast iron) brown the bacon on one side. Turn bacon and add the potatoes. Cook until nearly done, about 15 minutes. Add the onions or onions and chives, and cover to let them smother, about five minutes. Serve right from the skillet.

SMOTHERED POTATOES

This recipe just has bacon fat and no bacon, like the other. Bill Austin of Fort Madison, Iowa, makes this tasty dish.

3 T. bacon fat
1 c. onion slices
4 c. potato slices, peeled or unpeeled
seasonings to taste

In 10-inch skillet, melt bacon fat. Add onions, saute until tender. Stir in potatoes and seasonings. Cover, continue cooking stirring occasionally until tender.

GREEN BEANS WITH BACON

Helen Grainger contributed this simple but tasty recipe.

To some cooked green beans add the bacon grease and bacon bits, instead of butter. Some diced onion that has been cooked in the drippings makes them better. And, some savory added to it all makes them best.

HAM AND BEAN BAKE

Beans were one of the first successful canned products.

2 c. cooked ham, cubed	2 T. catsup
2-16 oz. cans pork and beans in tomato sauce	2 tsp. minced onion
	2 tsp. Worcestershire sauce
2 T. molasses	1 tsp. mustard

In mixing bowl combine all ingredients in order. Spoon into 6 individual casseroles, or one large one. Bake uncovered at 375° till hot, about 25 minutes.

MEXICO PINTO BEANS

Beans may not always go with chili, but Bernard F. Ederer, of Television Adventure Film fame, recommends them with a javelina barbecue, Gila Bend style. But don't wait till you serve spitted pig to taste these "pecos strawberries."

1 lb. pinto beans	1 tsp. salt, optional
6 c. water	2 T. bacon fat
½ tsp. cumin	2 red chili peppers
2 cloves garlic	

Cover beans with water and soak overnight. In the morning, drain; add cumin, garlic, and salt. Now add fat or ham with the chili peppers. Put in a bean jar; cover with hot water and bake for several hours, about 325°.

SQUASH FRITTERS

LaNelle E. Davis, of Broken Bow, Oklahoma, found recipes dated 1807 among her grandmother's belongings.

4-5 small yellow squash, grated	¼ tsp. salt, optional
3 eggs, beaten	½ tsp. cinnamon
4 T. flour	½ tsp. allspice

Combine all ingredients. Drop batter by tablespoon into a hot, buttered skillet. Smooth each into a fritter and cook until brown. Serve with maple syrup.

FRIED TURNIPS

Sometimes on the frontier the only fare for the day was turnips. Folks still enjoy turnips; George M. McCray, of Florence, Alabama, prefers them fried.

Boil sliced or chunked turnips in water for 5 minutes. Drain them, then batter them in flour, cornmeal or cracker meal, salt and pepper. Fry the turnips in butter till brown.

GREEN TOMATO GRAVY

When you grow your own tomatoes, like Helen Grainger, you can use the green ones. With cold chicken or other meat this dish makes a meal.

Slice a few green tomatoes and season them if you wish. Heat a frying pan with a generous amount of lard or oil and fry the floured tomato slices. When soft and brown, remove them from the pan. Add flour to grease; mix well. Add milk to gravy to made desired consistency, and cook until thick and blended. Pour over tomato slices.

GREEN BEANS WITH ONIONS

In the "good old days," according to Naomi Wood, of Dover, Arkansas, most women would have been ashamed to buy any canned goods other than tomatoes or corn at the store. They raised their own. No woman wanted to be called "a can opener cook."

2 T. oil or vegetable shortening
½ c. chopped onions
1 pt. home-canned green beans (or the can opener variety)

Put oil in a heavy skillet; add onions and fry over medium heat till limp but not brown. Add green beans. Bring to a boil, and simmer till juice is evaporated. Serve with tortillas or thin slices of hot corn bread.

SWEET 'N SOUR LETTUCE

On their well-planned trip to the Great Salt Lake the Mormons moved in small groups. The first group plowed the fields and planted crops and gardens for those who followed. That progressive gardening allowed later followers to harvest the crops and plant new ones. The gardens grew leaf lettuce, which was prepared in pioneer lettuce salad.

To a mixture of lettuce and other greens, add a dressing made of equal parts of cream and herb vinegar, with sugar to sweeten to your taste.

COLE SLAW

LaVerne E. Ray, of Yuba City, California, enjoys this special cabbage salad. It could have stimulated an Old West cabbage patch craze.

1 head of cabbage cut in fine threads (do not use heart)
boiling water for the steamer
2 hard boiled eggs, chopped fine
1 tsp. to 1 T. curry powder or catsup
1 c. vinegar
seasonings

Put the cabbage in a steamer over boiling water two minutes; then lay it in a deep dish. Add the eggs. Heat together the curry powder or catsup, vinegar, salt and pepper. Pour sauce over cabbage.

OKLAHOMA SLAW

Lenora Taylor of historic Tahlequah, Oklahoma, home of Cherokee Heritage Center, favors a meal of this slaw with beans and cornbread.

½ c. vinegar
¾ c. salad oil
1 tsp. dry mustard
1 tsp. celery seed
½ c. sugar
1 large head of cabbage, shredded
1 large onion, shredded

Mix the vinegar, oil, mustard and celery seed. Pour the sugar on the cabbage and onion. Do not stir. Heat the vinegar and oil mixture to a boil. Pour over cabbage mixture; do not stir. Cover and refrigerate for at least 4 hours. Stir the slaw when ready to eat. It will keep several days in the refrigerator.

SAUERKRAUT SALAD

Old world ethnic and new world southwestern merge in this recipe from Lenora Taylor.

1 large 16 oz. can kraut,
  drained or 2 c. homemade
2 c. celery, chopped
½ c. onion, chopped
½ c. bell pepper, chopped
½ c. pimiento or
  purple cabbage, chopped
¾ c. vinegar
1½ c. sugar

Combine all the vegetables. The pimiento makes for a better flavor than does the purple cabbage. Mix vinegar and sugar and heat. Let cool and pour over the other ingredients. Let stand 24 hours in refrigerator.

CONDIMENT CORNER

CURRY POWDER

Here is a recipe from the days when westerners blended their own spices.

1 T. China turmeric
1 tsp. cassia
1 tsp. black pepper
1 tsp. cayenne
2 T. coriander seeds,
  pounded fine in a mortar

Mix all ingredients well and sift.

SOUTHWEST CHILI SAUCE

1 8-oz. can tomato sauce
½ tsp. ground cumin
1 T. red chili powder
1 large clove garlic,
  finely chopped
½ tsp. oregano
dried onions or
onion powder to taste

Combine all ingredients and mix well.

CHILI GRAVY

John Norwood says you should never add dry chili powder to a dish, as it will scorch and not have that good chili flavor. Instead, always soak it awhile in hot water or other liquid called for in your recipe.

John's delicious chili gravy will add flavor to any meat.

1 T. more or less
  chili powder
1 c. beef stock
2 c. flour
½ meat drippings

Warm stock and stir in chili powder. Allow to soak several minutes. Meanwhile mix flour and meat drippings in a pan at low heat, stirring constantly until golden brown. Add stock and chili powder mixture. Simmer until thick. (If gravy becomes too thick, it can be thinned by adding a little more stock.)

LEMON EXTRACT

With a little help from the peel, brandy could yield lemon extract. Cut off the yellow part of the rind and store in a wide-mouthed bottle half full of brandy. A pint bottle of brandy goes a long way.

FLAVORED VINEGARS

Tarragon, sweet basil, celery, horseradish, chili, raspberry, and burnt vinegar were but a few items used to flavor vinegar. Steep the herb or fruit in the heated vinegar. Bottle and store it until it is flavored. Strain. (A few herb sprigs may be left in the vinegar to make it look attractive.) Use bottles of various sizes. Use a handful of herbs for each pint, 2 for each quart.

If you heat the vinegar, it will develop the herbal flavor in several weeks. You may add herbs to room temperature vinegar. It will take a month to develop the full flavor.

MUSTARD

To dry mustard add salt, mix slowly with boiling water, rubbing a long time with knife or wooden spoon.

4 T. mustard
1 tsp. salt
2 T. water

CATSUP

Tomato catsup did not appear until after this condiment had been made with oysters, walnuts, anchovies, and other ingredients.

Mrs. Beeton's **Walnut Ketchup** is a very old recipe, over 100 years old. It became popular in the 1880s.

100 walnuts, gathered green, roughly chopped
1 handful salt
1 qt. vinegar
¼ oz. mace, ground
¼ oz. nutmeg, ground
¼ oz. cloves, ground
¼ oz. ginger, ground
¼ oz. whole black peppercorns
20 shallots, peeled
¼ lb. anchovies
1 pt. port wine

Put the walnuts in a jar or bowl with the salt and vinegar. Let them stand for eight days, stirring every day.

Drain the liquor from the walnuts and combine it and all remaining ingredients in a saucepan. Bring to a boil and simmer for about half an hour. If desired, strain. Adjust proportions of wine and vinegar to taste. Store in sterilized jars.

ALMOND FLAVORING

Save peach pits and dry for 1 day. Store to use as bitter almonds in flavoring custards, creams, and cakes. Plum stones are good, too.

PERKY-PORKY BARBECUE SAUCE

Whether you're barbecuing a pig, a cow, or a chicken, this barbecue sauce will add a touch of the old West.

3 lemons, juice and zest (peel)
3 onions chopped
3 c. catsup
1 c. Worcestershire sauce
3 tsp. chili powder
1 small can chopped chili peppers

Combine all ingredients. Use as a basting sauce or a marinade.

PRESERVING ROOT VEGETABLES

Walt Thayer still remembers the root cellar. Try his method of preserving surplus vegetables in a cool cellar.

Put a six-inch layer of clean sand with no pebbles in the bottom of a 40 or 50 gallon barrel or earthen crock. Cut the tops off beets, carrots, turnips, or rutabagas and lay them on their sides on the sand, but don't let them touch. If you do the vegetables will rot. Add another layer of sand so that at least two or three inches of sand covers vegetables. Repeat this procedure until the container is nearly full; then put at least four inches of sand over the top layer of vegetables and keep in a cool cellar. The vegetables will stay fresh all winter and the sand can be re-used for at least two seasons.

These vegetables and even apples can also be stored in "pits" with frost proof covers, but you get a higher percentage of spoilage, especially in apples.

FOOD AND FRIENDS

Herbs and spices season better than salt. Since rules are sometimes made to be broken, use your imagination, not just this chart. Let your taste buds have some power...

Beef: Basil, bay leaves, caraway, cayenne, celery seeds, chervil, chili powder, curry powder, dill weed, garlic powder, ginger, marjoram, onion powder, oregano, parsley, rosemary, sage, savory, tarragon, and thyme.

Pork: Basil, caraway, cinnamon powder, coriander, dill weed, fennel, garlic, marjoram, mustard, oregano, paprika, rosemary, sage, savory, tarragon and thyme.

Veal and Lamb: Basil, chervil, cinnamon, dill, garlic, ginger, marjoram, mint, oregano, paprika, rosemary, sage, savory, tarragon, and thyme.

Poultry: Basil, bay, celery, chervil, chives, coriander, dill, ginger, lemon balm, marjoram, nutmeg, paprika, rosemary, saffron, sage, tarragon, and thyme.

Fish and Shellfish: Anise, basil, bay, celery, chervil, chives, cloves, dill, fennel, lemon balm, mace, marjoram, paprika, parsley, pepper, rosemary, sage, savory, tarragon, and thyme.

Soups, Chowders and Stews: Anise seed, basil, bay, caraway, celery flakes or seed, chervil, chives, cloves, dill, fennel, marjoram, oregano, paprika, parsley, rosemary, sage, savory, tarragon, and thyme.

Eggs: Basil, cayenne, celery, chervil, chili powder, lemon balm, marjoram, oregano, paprika, parsley, rosemary, savory, tarragon, thyme, and turmeric.

Vegetables: Allspice, anise seed, basil, bay, caraway, celery, chervil, chives, cumin, curry powder, dill, fennel, marjoram, mint, mustard, parsley, rosemary, sage, tarragon, and thyme.

MILK BUCKETS, BUTTER CHURNS, AND EGG BASKETS

    A cow was an important creature on a frontier homestead. If twice-a-day milkings were begun as soon as the cow bore a calf and became "fresh," she could produce enough milk through the late spring, summer, and early fall to feed her calf and keep a growing family in milk, butter, and cheese. When cold weather came and fodder was less plentiful, the cow was allowed to go dry. Knowing this you can appreciate the ingenuity of dividing up one cup of milk (and one egg) equally among family members by making lumpy dick, a pioneer pudding, and you can understand the need for making a bread spread from goose fat.

    Raising chickens for eggs was not easy, what with hawks, weasels, and foxes. If successful, there would be pullets in the summer. Next year the pullets would begin laying; then there would be eggs to set. The following year there would be cockerels to fry, and more pullets to increase the flock. Then there would be eggs to eat. When the hens grew too old to lay eggs, there was chicken pie.

    The milk used originally in these recipes was probably not pasteurized. Pasteurization kills the germs that cause fermenting and give milk its sour power. Old fashioned raw buttermilk and raw sour milk were different from today's buttermilk. But the modern buttermilk will still furnish the acid often needed to react with baking soda.

    The cream today is often not "the cream of the crop." If you can invert a container of cream today without its moving, then you know what old fashioned heavy cream is. Otherwise, be content with what is labeled as heavy cream. It certainly beats what's in second place.

    Perhaps the pleasure we take in butter is not only a culinary one, but also one of nostalgia. Butter, basically a simple food, makes us feel that we still have a link with nature. Let's preserve the nostalgia and use real butter in these recipes.

CHAPTER 7
Cluck and Cream
Eggs and Dairy Products

CALIFORNIA ZEPHYR FRENCH TOAST

John Norwood worked on the railroad for fifty years. An Old West culinary expert, he submitted this recipe for French toast as it was served on the famed California Zephyr. It was never sprinkled with powdered sugar as in most restaurants but served with warm honey or maple syrup. Most people ate it with a side of ham, bacon, or sausage patty.

4 slices old white bread
3 eggs
½ tsp. nutmeg
2 tsp. flour
½ tsp. baking powder

Whip up 3 eggs with a chef's whip or beater until creamy but not frothy. Add the nutmeg, flour and baking powder. Grease well but do not saturate griddle and put over medium heat. Dip a piece of bread into the mixture. When you lift it from the egg mixture, let it finish dripping. Put it on the griddle. Dip a second slice of bread and lay it on top of the first one. Lift the bottom slice often to check. When it has reached a deep golden brown, turn the two slices together and cook the top side.

You will have a thick, delicious slice of French toast.

Bacon and Railroad French Toast (California Zephyr)

TANSY OMELETTE

Tansy is an old-fashioned herb that you can grow in your garden. If you are lucky enough to have some, you can make this omelette.

Tansy and eggs go well together. Use as much of the herb as suits your taste.

Prepare tansy by chopping. Beat 6 eggs with a fork. Stir in the tansy, and season to taste. Pour the mixture into a greased skillet or omelette pan. When the bottom is set and the top is creamy, turn or cover, so that the top is cooked. It should take about 2 minutes to complete the cooking. Serve at once.

PIPERADE

The Basques know how to combine fresh vegetables and eggs to make a special omelette.

⅔ c. olive oil
6 cloves garlic, minced
2 large onions
1 large green pepper, chopped
1 large red bell pepper, chopped
1 tender leek,
  cut into thin ridges
  including some of the greens
3 green onions,
  chopped

2 or 3 tomatoes, chopped
2 c. ham, diced
½ c. parsley, minced
1 tsp. dried basil, minced
1 scant pinch of thyme
pinch of mint
½ tsp. sugar
freshly ground pepper,
  to taste
6 eggs

Heat the olive oil and saute the garlic and onions in it until tender. Add the peppers, leek, green onions, tomatoes, and ham. Toss gently. Reduce the heat and cook until the liquid from the tomatoes is reduced to a sauce. Add herbs, pepper, and sugar.

Beat eggs and pour into vegetable mixture. Do not scramble in standard fashion. Allow to sit a moment or two until egg on bottom of pan begins to set. With spatula or wooden spoon, pull the ingredients to side of pan, tilting pan, let the raw egg run into the empty space. Continue doing this until all the egg is lightly cooked.

HOPI OMELETTE

This dish will stick to your ribs! If you can't find the canned cactus leaf, it just won't be a Hopi omelet. There is really no substitute, so if you can't get canned cactus leaf, just call it a cottage cheese omelet. Some gourmet produce departments offer fresh cactus leaf.

1 onion, diced
4 cloves of garlic,
  finely minced
4 eggs

½ c. canned cactus leaf, drained
½ c. cottage cheese
oregano and pepper to taste

In a heavy pan saute the onion and garlic in oil or drippings.

Beat the eggs and pour into a large omelet pan. Spoon the sauteed onion and garlic over the eggs. Add the cactus and cottage cheese. Sprinkle lightly with oregano and pepper. When the egg has formed a skin on the bottom, fold in half and continue cooking until the egg is set. Serve with steamed flour tortillas or fry bread.

PUEBLO HOMINY AND EGGS

This dish is still enjoyed by the Indians of the Southwest.

2 T. oil or drippings	1 c. country-style
1 chopped onion	mild chili sauce
4 cloves of garlic,	chilies and other seasonings
finely minced	to taste
1 sweet pepper,	6 eggs
cut into thin strips	sliced tomato
1-16 oz. can hominy, drained	watercress or parsley

In a heavy skillet melt the oil or drippings. Saute the onion and garlic. Add the pepper and saute a minute longer. Add the hominy and the chili sauce. Let simmer until hot. Add the chilies and other seasonings, if desired. In a separate skillet fry the eggs to your liking. Arrange the eggs and hominy on plates, garnished with tomatoes, watercress, and parsley.

FILLIN

In the good ol' days milk and eggs came from cows and chickens. When the cow was giving milk and the chickens were laying eggs, dishes such as fillin could be made. Eggs with onions star in this 1906 recipe, a favorite of Ellen E. Pope of Bowman, North Dakota.

¼ lb. butter	6 eggs
2 large onions,	½ c. sweet cream
slice or dice	salt and pepper to taste

Beat eggs and cream together with seasonings. Pour over onions in pan of melted butter and cook until they are soft, stirring occasionally.

Serve as a breakfast dish or an accompaniment to supper.

HANGTOWN FRY

Hang Town Fry is perhaps the most famous of all gold camp victuals. Hang Town, now known as Placerville, is a Mother Lode town in the lower elevations of the Sierra Nevada foothills. This recipe will serve 1 miner or 4 to 5 others.

1 T. butter	1 bell pepper, cut into
1 T. vegetable oil	thin strips
1 onion, chopped	6 slices of bacon
2 or 3 garlic cloves,	12 oysters, shelled
finely minced	8 eggs

Melt the butter and vegetable oil in an iron skillet. Saute the onion until transparent but not browned. Add garlic. Toss the pepper with the onions and the garlic until partially cooked. Remove the vegetables to another plate and fry the bacon until crisp. Set the bacon aside.

Saute quickly the oysters. While the oysters are cooking, lightly beat the eggs. Return the vegetables to the pan with the oysters. Crumble the bacon over this mixture. Pour in the eggs. When the eggs have somewhat set, gently pull the cooked egg to one side and tilt the pan; let the remaining raw egg run down the pan. Continue doing this until all the egg is set. Season to taste.

OLD TIME BUTTER MAKING

Walt Thayer remembers old-fashioned butter making. Warm weather was bad for making butter. One method of rendering butter firm and solid in hot weather was to use carbonate of soda and alum powder. For 20 pounds of butter 1 tsp. each of soda and powdered alum were mixed together at the time of churning and added to the cream. This made the butter firm and solid and gave it a clean, sweet flavor. Sometimes family members took turns at the churn before the butter was finished.

One way of storing the butter once it was made was to wrap it in cornhusks. The husks were carefully removed from the ears, then scalded and dried in the sun. When dry, the husks were dipped in ice water and carefully opened. Well-rinsed butter was worked into the shape of corn ears and placed inside the husks. The layers of the husk were folded back together, tied up tight, and placed in "pickle juice."

The pickling liquid contained ½ lb. of salt, 1 oz. of saltpetre, ½ lb. of sugar, and 3 qts. of water. This mixture was heated to scalding temperature, then skimmed and cooled in a large barrel or crock.

The very last step was to make sure that all of the butter-filled husks were weighted down and completely covered with pickling liquid. If properly prepared, this butter would keep for a year. "A lot of work," says our old time butter maker, "but it tasted so much better than today's butter—or margarine." Walt's family kept some of their butter in the cool water of a spring near the house. Some families even had a springhouse of their own.

SMIERKASE—COTTAGE CHEESE

Back in the days when Paul Brunner was a kid, cheese made from sour or clabbered milk was known by many names; **cottage cheese** was one, but his family called it **smierkase**.

1 qt. sour milk	1 T. butter
salt	rich cream

Scald the milk until the whey rises to the top. Then put the curd in a cheesecloth bag. Do not squeeze the bag. Hang it to drain, about 5-6 hours. When it is dry, you can salt it and work it, molding and kneading with the hands. Add the butter and just enough cream to make cheese of a fine texture.

BIRD'S NEST PUDDING

This custard coupled with apples is a specialty of Californian Judith Michaels.

apples to fill a dish	1 qt. milk
sugar to suit your sweet tooth, about ¼ lb.	8 eggs

Pare and core as many apples as will stand in a dish. Fill the holes with sugar. Make a custard with the milk, eggs and sugar. Pour it over the top and bake one hour in a 350° oven.

BEE BALM PUDDING

Grow, beg, borrow, or steal this herb for tea and this recipe.

1 ⅔ c. milk
½ c. brown sugar
1 T. butter, softened
1 tsp. vanilla
2 eggs
2 c. rice, cooked
⅓ c. leaves from bee balm plant finely chopped
1 c. sugar cookie crumbs
½ tsp. lemon rind, grated
1 tsp. lemon juice

Preheat oven to 325°. Combine milk, brown sugar, butter, vanilla, and eggs. Beat well and mix with rice. Set aside. Combine balm leaf, cookie crumbs, lemon rind and juice. Decorate with the flowers from the plant.

GINGER-PEACHY ICE CREAM

Ice cream was not so easily available a century ago as it is today, but it was better. You can make this spicy fruity ice cream with an old-fashioned churn. Even if you cheat a bit and use a modern ice cream freezer, it will still beat the supermarket variety!

4 c. pureed peaches
5 c. heavy cream
¼ c. candied ginger, finely chopped
1¾ c. sugar
4 eggs
vanilla extract

Combine pureed peaches with cream and ginger. Beat eggs, gradually adding sugar. Continue to beat until mixture is very stiff. Add cream mixture and vanilla extract to your taste. Pour into gallon container and freeze.

To make your own candied ginger, cut up a large, clean ginger root in bite-size pieces, and simmer in ½ lb. of sugar or honey.

MAKE BELIEVE LEMON PIE

An imitation "lemon" pie using buttermilk could fool more pioneers than even the famous imitation apple pie. When you are sixty miles, from a lemon this version makes a wonderful imitation, according to Ellen Pope.

2 c. sugar
4 T. flour
4 egg yolks
4 egg whites
2 c. buttermilk
1 T. lemon extract
1 T. butter
1 9-inch pie shell
pinch of cream of tarter

Beat together sugar, flour, and egg yolks and one egg white. Add buttermilk, extract, and butter. Pour into shell. Bake at 350° until filling just quivers in the center when shaken gently.

For the meringue combine remaining three egg whites with a pinch of cream of tartar. Beat until stiff. Spread the meringue over the pie and brown under the broiler or in a very hot oven.

BAKED ALASKA

For a grande touch when the living is good . . . Baked Alaska was often featured in elegant restaurants or as part of railroad fare.

1 qt. brick-style ice cream	½ tsp. cream of tartar
5 egg whites	⅔ c. sugar
1 tsp. vanilla	

Trim cake 1 inch longer on all sides than brick of ice cream; place cake on plate. Center ice cream on cake. Cover; freeze firm. At serving time, beat egg whites with vanilla and cream of tartar till soft peaks form. Gradually add sugar, beating till stiff peaks form.

Transfer cake with ice cream to baking sheet; spread with egg white mixture, sealing to edges of cake all around the four sides. Swirl for peaks. Bake at 500° till golden, about 3 minutes. Slice and serve immediately. Makes 8 servings.

Tansy flowers and leaves flavored egg and dairy dishes.

PRESERVING THE PAST

Before canning was invented every cook had to master drying and pickling food. Salting, pickling, and corning were variations on the same technique. All used great quantities of salt and "put the meat down" in the cellar or in broth. Beef, pork and legs of lamb were salted. Pork was pickled and beef was corned.

Many small, young vegetables were pickled. Homemade apple cider was essential for pickling. The process of making vinegar could be speeded up by adding "mother of vinegar"—the brown mat of bacteria in old vinegar or cider. It was removed when the vinegar was the right strength. Nuts and seeds also went into spicy brine.

For all the potent vinegar, pickled food frequently spoiled. To prevent spoilage jars or crocks were plugged tightly with a cork or covered with a pig's bladder. They were not hermetically sealed, and the upper third was apt to spoil.

Before scientists knew pectin in apples made sweetened fruit syrup set up or that heat processing would save food in a can, putting up was otherwise limited to making jams and preserves. Sugar was the preservative; otherwise chemicals were added. Jams and preserves were stored in clean, unsterilized glasses or pots and sealed by fitting a piece of brandy-soaked paper on the surface of the fruit. Paraffin came later as a by-product of kerosene.

Once the effect of heat on bacteria was understood, canning techniques improved. John Mason's jar in 1858 helped. A rubber gasket fitted the shoulder on the Mason jar, and a zinc lid screwed down tight.

The pantry, the root cellar, the smokehouse, the springhouse—all held treasures of preserved food in the Old West.

CHAPTER 8
Preservation
Relishes and Preserves

CANNING CUES

Sterilize the jars: Wash them well and boil them in water to cover for 15 minutes, either in one large kettle or several smaller ones. Include lids, funnel, and utensils in the bath. Let them remain in hot water, removing as needed with sterile tongs.

Test for doneness: Too little cooking makes the fruit in jam and jelly runny; too much makes it chewy. Monitor the cooking with a candy thermometer, and stop when it reaches 222°. Or use grandmother's "sheeting" test: Hold the coated stirring spoon horizontally over the pot. At first the syrup will drip from the edge. After enough cooking, the drips will unite and fall from the spoon in a thin sheet.

Fill the sterilized jars by ladling in the hot food until almost full, using a wide-mouth funnel for jam or jelly. The jars or glasses should be straight-sided for easy sealing. Smaller ones are better, because they empty quickly. The refrigerator will keep large opened quantities, but chilling reputedly dulls the preserved flavor.

Seal the jars: The old custom was to cover the fruit with circles of letter paper soaked in brandy. Over this cover and the container edge another paper would be fastened with glue, or a moist animal bladder would be tied to shrink taut as it dried. With food preserved in pickling brine this was not necessary. You can use paraffin to seal. Apply paraffin in two layers—the first one on the hot contents, the second after the first has cooled. Remember that it is flammable; follow directions on the package. Label and store jars properly. Give the contents and date of each jar. Store away from heat and light.

About pickling: Never use copper vessels for pickling. Enameled kettles are best for cooking acid solutions. Do not store pickles in earthenware vessels. Before glass jars became abundant and cheap, wooden barrels and stoneware crocks were the recommended containers.

IMITATION MAPLE SYRUP

12 corn cobs
4 c. water or enough to cover
4 c. sugar

To put up some "maple syrup" from corn cobs, here is a recipe from Mrs. Mary Anne McDonald, of Saskatchewan, Canada. The cobs give the maple flavor. Use equal measures of sugar and water.

Boil clean corn cobs in water; then remove the cobs and add brown sugar; boil to a nice, thick syrup. You can hardly tell this from genuine maple syrup.

Preserving nature's bounty

WILD PLUM JAM

One of the most delicious of the wild fruits found near rivers and streams in various parts of the Southwest is the wild plum. Red and yellow varieties were plentiful in the Old West. Although sweet when fully ripe, the wild plum has a high acid content that makes it good for jellies and preserves. For all of these recipes from Davilla Bright you should first cover the plums with water and boil until skins break and the fruit is tender.

4 lbs. fresh plums	1 box powdered pectin
½ c. water	8 c. water

Wash plums, remove pits, and chop pulp. Place in 6-quart kettle with water. Simmer covered for 5 minutes. Remove cover, add powdered pectin, and bring to a rapid boil, stirring rapidly all the while. Add sugar and bring to a full rolling boil, stirring constantly. Boil for 1 minute. Remove from heat. Skim off foam and continue to stir and skim by turns for 5 minutes, to cool slightly. Ladle into hot sterilized jars. Seal.

PLUM JELLY

Drain off liquid from boiled plums. Add one cup of sugar for each cup of juice. Bring to a boil, stirring constantly for three to five minutes. When drops slide off spoon in a sheet, jelly is done. Pour in glasses or jars and seal with melted paraffin, or put into jars with new lids that seal.

PLUM PRESERVES

The difference between preserves and jam is that in preserves the fruit is nearly whole and in jam it is in small bits. Grandmother thought that plum seeds gave the jam or preserves an especially good flavor so that she left in some pits.

3 lbs. plums,
 washed, with stems and
 blossom ends removed

4 c. sugar
1½ c. water

Prick each plum several times with fork. Combine sugar and water; bring to boil. Add plums; simmer until fruit is clear and tender and syrup sheets from spoon. Pack into hot sterilized jars and seal.

PLUM BREAD PUDDING

This recipe can be made with fresh or preserved plums. It is good for using the leftover plums from the plum jelly.

3 c. sliced plums
¾ to 1 c. sugar
½ ground cinnamon
1 T. fresh lemon juice or
 vinegar
2 tsp. cornstarch
1 T. cold water

¼ tsp. vanilla extract
6 or 7 slices of bread
butter
ground cinnamon
 for sprinkling
whipped cream, optional

Combine plums with sugar, cinnamon, and juice or vinegar. Dissolve cornstarch in water. Add vanilla. Mix the plums with the cornstarch. Arrange the bread in a baking pan. Dot with butter and sprinkle with cinnamon. Bake in 350° oven for about 30 minutes. Serve with whipped cream.

PIEPLANT PRESERVES

Pieplant is another name for rhubarb. Besides using these preserves as a topping for bread, pancakes, waffles, or ice cream, you can bake them into a pie.

2 qt. rhubarb, cut in ½-inch pieces
4 c. sugar

Mix fruit and sugar; let stand for one hour. Bring to a boil and cook rapidly for about 30 minutes, or until the rhubarb mixture is thick. Stir frequently to prevent burning. Turn into hot fruit jars and seal, or put in jelly glasses and seal with paraffin. Makes about four 8-ounce glasses.

LEMON BALM JELLY

4 c. water
1 c. lemon balm
1 box Sure-Jell or bottle Certo
sugar

Boil the water and add the balm. Steep and strain. Add the pectin, in powdered or liquid form, and 1 cup sugar per liquid. Boil hard 1 minute. Pour into glasses and seal.

MULBERRY JELLY

Mulberries are sweet to the taste, but you are going to have to be fast on foot, to beat the birds to them. Billy Jack Tabor's simple suggestions for making jelly start with using one part juice to one part sugar. Then boil to the jelly stage.

For jam, simmer the berries in their own juice until tender. Add an equal amount of sugar and cook until thick.

Mulberries make delicious dumplings and pies, too. So let's go 'round the mulberry juice.

HONEY WITHOUT BEES

The Indians called bees "white man's flies." As the Indians showed whites how to obtain maple syrup, however, whites showed them how to obtain honey. When the pioneers did not raise bees, sugar, clover, and rose blossoms would do the trick. Daisy Leist of Fargo, North Dakota, makes honey without bees, just as her family has been doing for years. And it's something to buzz about!

45 red clover blossoms
45 white clover blossoms
  (substitute 90 of one
  or the other)

25 wild rose blossoms
10 c. sugar
1 c. water
1 tsp. powdered alum

Mix and boil exactly three minutes. Strain through a tightly woven dish cloth. This makes 2 quarts of delicious honey.

PICCALILLI

Ben Sweet's recipe is from a household notebook owned by a nearby rancher and dated 1899. Ben, who lives in Henderson, Nevada, says that the leather bound book includes various home remedies as well as recipes.

1 peck green tomatoes,
1 large cabbage, chopped
1 dozen onions, chopped
½ pint salt
vinegar to cover

6 medium to large green
  peppers, seeded and
  chopped fine
½ T. each of cloves, allspice,
  pepper, dry mustard

Combine tomatoes, cabbage, and onions; put the salt on them, and let it all stand overnight. Drain off the brine; rinse, and scald in weak vinegar, then drain again. Add the peppers and the spices.

Pack into sterilized jars and seal.

CHOKECHERRY AND GOOSEBERRY RELISH

Relishes and preserves added colorful vegetables and fruits to the bleak pioneer diet. They were especially "relished" in the winter.

1 lb. gooseberries
1 lb. chokecherries
½ c. cider vinegar

½ tsp. salt
¼ tsp. each allspice,
  cinnamon and cloves

Combine all ingredients except spices in saucepan. Mix well. Cook over medium heat for 30-40 minutes, stirring frequently. Add spices about 10 minutes before cooking time is up. Pack in hot, sterilized jars. Store in cool place.

MOM'S CHOW-CHOW

Davilla Bright's mother made this tasty chow chow.

½ gal. green tomatoes
½ gal. cabbage
½ doz. green peppers
½ doz. onions

1 gal. vinegar
2 lbs. sugar
1 T. powdered nutmeg
1 tsp. cloves

Grind or chop vegetables and place in a large strainer or bag, set over a pot sprinkling a little salt on each layer. Drain overnight. Then rinse off the salt.

Combine vinegar, sugar, nutmeg and cloves in large open kettle. Add vegetables and cook about ½ hour until tender. Can from the kettle while the vegetables are very hot. (Adding a few drops of green cake coloring keeps the chow-chow looking green and fresh.)

SAUERKRAUT

Harriet Davis uses an old recipe for making sauerkraut.

Take a strong wooden vessel that will not leak and is large enough to hold sufficient sauerkraut for the consumption of a large family over the winter. Take off the green leaves from the cabbage heads and chop the cabbage into small pieces. Press them to fit closely into the cask, and scatter over them a handful of salt until the cask is full. Cover the cask, and place a heavy weight on it. Let it stand in a warm place for four or five days.

Then remove the cask to a cool place and keep it always covered up. Anise seed, strewed among the layers in the course of preparation, adds a peculiar and agreeable flavor.

When serving the kraut, boil it for one to two hours.

TOMATO PRESERVES

This old cowboy recipe was also used by the native New Mexicans. "It's the only way I ever knew of eating tomatoes," says Naomi Wood, who never puts tomatoes in her chili.

1 No. 2 can tomatoes chopped
—20 oz. tomatoes, drained
or 1 lb. fresh plus 4 oz. liquid

1 c. sugar

Empty tomatoes into a stew pot. Add sugar. Stir and bring to a boil. Reduce heat and simmer for about 30 minutes.

BELL PEPPER RELISH

This relish probably preserved the last of summer's bounty, harvested before the first fall frost. The lady of the house hoped to make enough to last through spring. It served the Bright family many years.

6 lbs. green and red peppers
3 medium onions
2 tsp. mustard seeds

3 T. salt
3 c. sugar
3 c vinegar

Grind or chop the peppers and onions fine and add the mustard seed and salt. Heat the vinegar and sugar mixture. When the water boils, add the vegetables and cook 10 minutes. Put in jars and seal. This makes about 7 pints.

LARGE GREEN PEPPERS STUFFED WITH PICKLED CABBAGE

In 1857 the grandmother of Harriet Davis, Phoenix, Oregon, picked a peck of peppers and stuffed them with pickled cabbage.

1 peck large green peppers
1 large cabbage
12 large onions
4-5 young cucumbers
2 oz. mustard seed

1 oz. each allspice, ginger and cinnamon
½ oz. cloves
vinegar

Cut out pepper stems. Carefully scrape out the peppers and lay them with stems in salt and water for several days. Wash them well in cold water; then lay them to drain.

Prepare the cabbage as for cole slaw, cutting very fine. Mince the onions very fine. Cut the cucumbers in very small pieces. Mix the onions and cucumbers together and add the spices. Scald this mixture in vinegar to cover. Then cool the mixture.

Fill the peppers as full as possible; then sew on the stems, or the pieces you have cut out. Put peppers in jars and fill with cold, strong vinegar.

Pickled Peppers

PICKLED BEETS

The families of Laura Ingalls Wilder and of Geraldine Duncann both made pickled beets using a similar recipe.

10 beets
1½ c. white vinegar
1 T. pickling spices
⅓ T. salt
½ c. sugar

Wash beets and boil until very tender. When cool enough to handle, slip off the skins. Trim and slice. Put into a bowl, crock or large glass jar. Strain the water the beets were cooked in and save.

Put the vinegar in a pan and add the pickling spices, salt and sugar. Bring to a boil, reduce heat and simmer 20 minutes. Pour over beets. If more liquid is needed to cover, add beet water.

These pickled beets will be ready to eat in about 3 days and will keep indefinitely in the refrigerator.

PICKLED EGG, OLD FASHIONED RECIPE

Both the old fashioned recipe and the modern one yield delicious pickled eggs.

Obtain a wide-mouth earthen jar to hold one dozen eggs. Let the eggs be boiled quite hard; when fully done, place the same, after taking them up, into a pan of cold water. Remove the shells and deposit the eggs carefully in the jar. Have on the fire a quart or more if necessary of good cider vinegar, into which you introduce one ounce of raw ginger, two or three blades of sweet mace, one ounce of allspice, half an ounce of whole black pepper, salt, half an ounce of mustard seed with four cloves of garlic. When it has simmered for half an hour, take it up and pour the contents into the jar, taking care to observe that the eggs are wholly covered. When quite cold, stopper it down for use. It will be ready after a month. When cut into quarters, the pickled eggs serve as a garnish and afford a nice relish to cold meat of any kind.

PICKLED EGG, MODERN RECIPE

12 eggs
4 c. vinegar
4 T. pickling spices, including
  nutmeg, mace, celery seed,
  mustard, cloves, cinnamon, salt

Boil as many eggs as you wish to pickle for 20 minutes. Shell them. Have ready scalded white vinegar containing the pickling spices.

When the vinegar is boiling hot, drop in the eggs and turn off the heat. Let them heat through for 10 minutes. Pack the eggs and the liquid at once into sterilized jars and seal. Keep in a cool place.

PICKLED CAULIFLOWER

6 small heads of cauliflower
  broken into flowerettes
salted water
1 gal. vinegar
½ lb. brown sugar
1 oz. whole peppercorns
1 oz. white mustard seed
1 oz. celery seed
1 oz. turmeric
½ oz. cloves

Boil the cauliflower in water to cover. Let the flowerettes scald until a broom straw can be run through them or a fork can easily pierce them; then skim out into jars. Combine the vinegar, sugar, and the spices; boil all together for twenty minutes, and while very hot pour over the cauliflower. Cover closely and it will keep all winter.

HAM

The root cellar, the spring house, and the smokehouse were important in the preservation of food. Mabel Bays, of Tulsa, Oklahoma, found tips on the curing, smoking and keeping of hams in old Arizona newspapers.

"To a cask of hams, say 25-30, after having packed them closely and sprinkled them slightly with salt, let them lie thus for 3 days; then make a brine sufficient to cover them, by putting salt into clear water, making it strong enough to bear up a sound egg or potato. Then add ½ pound of saltpetre, and a gallon of molasses; let them lie in the brine for 6 weeks—they are then exactly right. Take them up and let them drain; then while damp, rub the flesh side and the end of the leg with finely pulverized black, red, or cayenne pepper; let it be as fine as dust, and dust every part of the flesh side, then hang them up and smoke. You may leave them hanging in the smokehouse or other cool place where the rats cannot reach them, as they are perfectly safe from all insects; and will be a dish fit for a prince, or an American citizen."

PICKLED FISH

Meat wasn't the only preserved protein, fish was, too, as in this succulent recipe from Mrs. Neil Leist.

fish, enough to make 6
  cups of bite-size pieces
  (more than 1 fish, of course)
strong salt solution made of equal
  amounts of salt and water
1 c. white vinegar
1 c. sugar
1 T. mixed pickling spices

Skin and fillet fish but leave the rib. The vinegar will dissolve bones later. Cut into bite-size pieces.

Soak fish in strong salt solution for 48 hours. Salt solution should be strong enough to float an egg. Rinse fish and soak in white vinegar for 48 hours. Drain. Then mix sugar, vinegar, and spices. Thinly slice 1 onion and add to mixture. Pour mixture over the fish. You should have about 1½ quarts of fish and broth when you are through. Make sure the fish is covered with liquid. If you need to add more vinegar, add a proportional amount of sugar and spices.

Let stand at least 2 weeks before serving. One month is really better. Shake and stir every couple of days.

FANCY MINCEMEAT

Harriet Davis's mincemeat depends on a unique blend of citron, cider, plums, and lemons, along with brandy and wine.

2 lb. beef suet, chopped fine
2 lb. apples, cored,
  pared, chopped fine
3 lb. currants,
  washed and stemmed
1 lb. brown sugar
½ lb. citron,
  cut into thin slices
2 lb. roast beef,
  free from skin and gristle,
  chopped fine

2 nutmegs, grated
2 T. salt, more or less to taste
juice of 6 lemons,
  with grated rinds
½ pt. brandy,
  plus 1/8 cup
1 pt. sweet wine
1 qt. cider

Combine the suet, apples, currants, plums or raisins, sugar, citron, and meat in a large pan, strewing the spices as you work; mix the liquid ingredients and pour into the pan. Stir together. Cover the mincemeat closely, and set it away in a cold place. When needed, stir up the meat from the bottom. The suet will cook in the pie. Remove amount of mincemeat needed and add some brandy to remaining ingredients.

Mincemeat Makings

METHODIST MINCEMEAT

Mincemeat was originally an alternative to smoking or drying meat. This 1880 recipe was perfected by Grandmother Roberts and handed down to her grandchild Edith Pope, of Bowman, North Dakota. We call it Methodist because it contains no alcohol.

beef neck to yield 3 cups
1 c. suet
1 c. raisins
 and 1 c. currants
4-5 c. chopped dried
 or fresh apples
1 c. molasses
1 c. vinegar
3 c. beef broth
3 c. brown sugar
1 tsp. each cinnamon,
 cloves and nutmeg
2 tsp. salt, optional

Boil the meat and chop it. Chop the suet in a bowl and combine with the meat. Add the remaining ingredients. Add salt to the meat mixture while cooking. Cook for an hour until it thickens. Grandmother Roberts did most of her chopping in an old wooden bowl. The finished mincemeat can be packed in glass jars, sealed and put away as it is without processing.

If you don't have a cool spring house or root cellar you should put the jars of mincemeat in your refrigerator to store for long periods.

MINCE PIES

The Indians invented mincemeat with wild berries and nuts. When the pioneers did not have buffalo meat, they used beef from their cattle and put other goods things in a pie filling. Russell E. Hill, of Dillwyn, Virginia, whose western paintings hang in the White House and embassies around the world, found this recipe in a cracked and darkened 1874 cookbook, called **The Home Cook Book**.

Make the mincemeat filling at least 1 day before using in pies.

6 lb. lean beef,
 boiled tender and chopped fine
1 lb. beef suet
5 lb. apples, chopped
2 lb. raisins
2 lb. currants
½ T. cloves
1 T. allspice
1 T. salt
3 lb. brown sugar
1 qt. wine
1 qt. brandy
the liquor in which
 the meat was boiled

Combine all ingredients. Cook for an hour. Store in a stone jar or glass jar covered with a double paper and tied. When you fill pies add a little more wine and chopped apples.

SAVORY GOOSE SPREAD

Goose fat could be preserved and used as butter, according to Ellen Pope. It was better than no butter at all, but as one pioneer lady said, "You sure are happy when the cow comes fresh."

raw fat of a 12 lb. goose,
 cut in small pieces
2 onions, chopped
2 tart apples, chopped
1 tsp. marjoram dried
 or fresh sprig tied in a
 piece of cloth, cheesecloth,
 or sieve

WINTER SOUP

Snow was used to preserve soup during the North Dakota winters. Ellen Pope's ancestors knew they would have a hearty soup.

1 ham bone
1 lb. smoked sausage or bologna
½ lb. split yellow dried peas
½ lb. split green peas
2 large onions, cut lengthwise

2 T. oil, lard
  or other fat
1 c. milk or cream
  (evaporated milk will do)

Boil the ham bone with the sausage or bologna and split peas. Fry the onions in small amount (to barely cover the skillet) oil or lard until almost slightly burned and add them to the soup. Simmer the soup until the peas are soft. Peas may be sieved if desired. Gradually stir milk or cream into soup.

Winter soup can be made in an electric skillet.

SWEET SOMETHINGS

A lack of ingredients never prevented pioneers from preparing delicious desserts. Instead of lemon juice for lemon pie, the resourceful cook used homemade vinegar.

Apples, of course, went into pie, which was often served for breakfast. But homemakers also boiled apple cider down to a thick concoction used in cider pie. And dried apples found their way into the chuck wagon for a cowboy's dessert.

The sugar of the Old West was coarse, slightly brown and so hard it had to be loosened with a special auger and ground in a sugar mill. When white sugar was available, it was used for a special treat, like "topshelf" gingerbread. "Lowershelf gingerbread" meant everyday molasses gingerbread.

In the mid 1800s one of the newer products was vanilla extract. Ladies often substituted rose, geranium or tansy when vanilla was not available. Before extract, vanilla beans were cut up and used for flavor. Chocolate was usually available only as a drink, not in desserts.

Women leavened baked goods with sour milk and molasses or pearl ash or saleratus. Baking powder, available in the 1860s, was not widely accepted until much later. The 1880s witnessed a flood of new recipes for light baked goods.

Cornstarch was used to thicken desserts; more was used for molded puddings. Cornstarch manufacturers gave away fancy molds to encourage sales of their product.

Platters loaded with plenteous desserts always were the most popular dishes at church dinners. Society matrons presided at the cake table, while lesser lights served the other food. For a young man to escort a girl to one of these socials meant there would most likely be a wedding soon. Sometimes the church sponsored a pie social or an ice cream social featuring desserts instead of a whole meal.

Pioneers did not consume as much sugar as people today, but their naturally good desserts will still satisfy your twentieth century sweet tooth.

CHAPTER 9
The End Of the Trail
Desserts

PIES

Your favorite pie dough recipe will work for any of the pies in this chapter. If you don't have a favorite recipe or if you just want to try another, we'll start with a few good ones from the Old West.

PLAIN PASTRY SHELL
Recipe 1 (Makes 2 crusts)

2½ c. flour,
 plus extra for dusting
½ tsp. salt

⅔ c. lard
6 T. chilled water

Chill all ingredients. In bowl mix flour and salt. Spoon lard into flour and blend with fingers or pastry blender until uniformly coarse. Continue to toss and add ice water gradually, just until dough comes clean from sides of bowl and forms a ball. Chill before rolling.

Anything can go into a pie crust—apples, potatoes, vinegar, etc.

PLAIN PASTRY SHELL
Recipe 2 (1½ crusts—for a bottom crust and a top lattice.)

1⅔ c. flour,
 plus more for rolling out
½ c. fat

dash salt
4 T. cold water

Put the flour into a pan and work the fat into it. Work into a paste with just enough water to make it smooth. Divide the fat into 4 parts. When the mixture resembles bean-size peas, sprinkle with water. Flour it lightly and fold over the edges and roll again; repeat three times. Using very little flour and rolling very thin; use your hands as little as possible and keep the paste cool. Divide the paste into two parts before rolling the last time, for a two crust pie.

PLAIN PASTRY SHELL
Recipe 3 (for one nine-inch pie shell.)

1 c. sifted pastry flour
 or 1 c. all-purpose flour,
 minus 1 T., with an optional
 1 T. cornstarch to take its place

½ tsp. salt
4½ T. shortening
6-8 T. cold water to moisten

Have all ingredients at the same temperature. Add salt to flour and resift. Add shortening and "cut in" with 2 knives or pastry blender, until mixture has appearance of coarse meal; add water, 1 T. at a time while mixing with a knife or spatula into a stiff paste. Just when the paste rolls into a ball and cleans the bowl of flour and paste, enough water has been added. Lightly transfer paste to a slightly floured board; do not knead, but with floured fingers form quickly and lightly into dough. Roll out lightly from the center outward, spreading into desired thickness.

RICH PASTRY SHELL

2 c. all-purpose flour
 or pastry flour
1 tsp. salt
1½ tsp. sugar
1 egg yolk

7 T. unsalted butter
 very cold and cut into pieces
1½ tsp. cider vinegar
3 to 4 T. cold water

Combine flour, salt, and sugar. Add egg yolk and blend with a pastry blender or fork. Add butter and lard and mix with a pastry blender or two knives till the pieces are the size of small peas. Add the vinegar and water, a little at a time, until mixture forms a ball when lightly pressed together. Roll out as directed for pie crust.

TO ROLL OUT PIE CRUST

Flour a pastry cloth, marble slab, or board. With a floured rolling pin roll the dough from the center into a circle. Rotate the pastry by giving it a quarter turn each time. Don't overwork the dough. If a baked shell is required, roll pastry 1/8 inch thick. Fit into pie pan. Flute edges and prick with fork. Bake crust in preheated very hot oven (450°) for 10 - 12 minutes.

Nut Custard Pie

NUT CUSTARD PIE

Nuts were a staple in the pioneers' diet. Wild nuts were gathered and featured in all sorts of dishes from soup to nuts.

1 c. sugar
2 T. cornstarch
¼ tsp. salt
1 c. molasses
1 c. water
4 eggs, slightly beaten
1 tsp. vanilla
1 9-inch pastry shell baked for just 5 minutes
¾ c. nuts, such as butternuts, hickory nuts, pecans, etc. coarsely broken
whipped cream

In a medium saucepan over low to medium heat combine sugar, cornstarch and salt. Stir in molasses and water. Over heat stir till thickened and bubbly. Gradually stir hot mixture into eggs. Add vanilla. Fill the pie shell with the custard mixture. Arrange the nuts on top in a pleasing pattern. Bake the pie at 350° till a knife inserted just off-center comes out clean, about 30 minutes. Cool. Top with whipped cream.

RAISIN VINEGAR PIE

Vinegar pie became a holiday special with the addition of raisins. This easy to prepare dessert will win the respect of the people at your table. Turn back the pages of holidays past and prepare Billy Jack Tabor's special pie.

2 c. raisins
2 c. cold water
pinch of salt
2 eggs
1½ c. sugar
4 T. flour
4 T. melted butter
4 T. cider vinegar
pastry for 2-crust pie

Boil the raisins in water until tender. Drain. Add cold water to the other ingredients. Cook and stir until thickened. Cool. Pour into the pie shell. Put on the top crust. Cut 3 or 4 slits near the center. Bake at 450° for 10 minutes, then at 350° for thirty minutes, or until brown.

OSGOOD PIE

Vinegar was a versatile ingredient in the Old West. It plays a vital part in this pie from James Furry of Texas.

2 eggs, separated
½ c. sugar
1 T. butter
½ tsp. cinnamon
½ tsp. cloves
1½ tsp. vinegar
½ c. nuts
½ c. raisins

Beat egg yolks lightly; add sugar, butter, spices and vinegar. Beat egg whites stiff and mix into egg yolk mixture. Stir in nuts and raisins. Bake filling and crust at same time, about 30 minutes, at 350°.

VINEGAR PIE

La Verne E. Ray suggests topping off her pea sausage, Chapter 6, with this delicious vinegar pie.

2 eggs
1 c. sugar
2 heaping T. flour
2 T. vinegar
¾ c. cold water
good sprinkling of nutmeg
½ -1 tsp.
pie crust

Beat the eggs, sugar and flour together. Blend in the vinegar and water. Flavor with nutmeg, sprinkled on top and bake in a crust, about 30 minutes, until filling is firm, at 375°.

BLUEBERRY CREAM PIE

Kenneth Heffling's grandmother was a little girl when her mother and father went west by covered wagon in 1880. Since then this recipe has been handed down through the generations. You can pick your berries—wild, cultivated, fresh, frozen or canned, but Kenneth prefers the fresh blueberries from Spokane, Washington, where he lives.

10-inch pie shell, pre-baked
5 c. blueberries
2 c. water, plus 2 T.
2 c. sugar
4 T. cornstarch
2 c. heavy cream, whipped

Wash blueberries; remove stems and green berries. Place 4 cups of the drained berries in pie shell. In a saucepan, bring water and sugar to boil and add remaining 1 cup of the berries and the cornstarch mixed with 2 tablespoons cold water. Bring to a boil. Simmer 2 minutes, stirring until sauce is thickened. Pour sauce over blueberries and cool pie. Top with whipped cream.

The pioneers liked their pies less thick than we do today. They didn't use as much cornstarch; we added a little more when we made this pie. Originally, the recipe called for 2 tablespoons.

AIR PIE

Edith Scholey, of Prescott, Arizona, remembers the superb fruit produced on Verde River ranches, near Clarksdale, where her grandfather, Jim Foster, worked. Grandmother Foster impressed company with a lovely fresh fruit dessert called Air Pie, because of the enormous pockets of air in the meringue.

1 9" pie crust
3 c. fresh sliced peaches or other fruit, plus one sliced peach for decoration
1 T. cinnamon
2 T. butter
1 c. sugar or less if desired
pinch of salt

Fill unbaked crust with fruit; pears, plums, or apricots can be substituted for the peaches. (Should you use dried fruit, stew it until tender.) Add cinnamon, butter, and sugar, plus salt. Bake until the fruit is tender at 350° for 45-50 minutes. If you are going to serve immediately, add meringue. Otherwise, hold the pie in the refrigerator for no more than two days.

½ c. sugar
2 egg whites
dash salt

Beat egg whites stiff, but not dry, and gradually beat in the sugar. Spoon big dollops of meringue to cover entire pie, but do not spread. Bake in 425° oven until meringue is medium brown. Enjoy this pie with its enormous mouthfuls of air. Top each slice with a fresh peach slice

FRESH RASPBERRY PIE

When not writing about gems or visiting ghost towns, Don Getz, of Salt Lake City, Utah, likes to cook. One of his favorite desserts is this gem of a pie, with a haunting flavor.

6 T. lard
3 T. boiling water
1 c. flour, sifted
1 tsp. sugar for pastry,
  plus about ½ c. more for fruit
1/8 tsp. salt

3 c. fresh raspberries,
  plus a few extra berries
  for decorating
confectioner's sugar,
  for sweetening cream
1 c. heavy cream, sweetened and
  whipped

Mix lard and water together with an electric mixer, or by hand, like Great-grandma, until mixture is creamy and cool. Sift flour, sugar and salt together into a bowl. Add lard mixture and stir with a fork until a ball is formed.

Roll out the dough and fit it into a pie plate. Trim and flute edges as desired. Prick bottom and sides, and bake at 450° for about 10-12 minutes or until lightly browned. Cool thoroughly.

Fill cooled pastry shell with chilled, cleaned, fresh raspberries and sprinkle with the sugar. Top with the sweetened, whipped cream and serve.

APPLESAUCE CUSTARD PIE

Whatever was available in the orchards or on the vines determined the kind of pie to be made.

Line a 9″ pie dish with dough for flaky crust and set aside.

Applesauce

2 c. tart apples,
  peeled and chopped
1½ c. sugar
1 tsp. powdered cinnamon

½ tsp. powdered ginger or
  fresh ginger root, minced
¼ tsp. ground nutmeg
½ c. apple brandy

Combine all ingredients in a large saucepan. Cook over medium heat until apples are quite soft. Mash with a potato masher and continue cooking over low heat until a thick butter results, about ½ hour.

Custard

2 c. extra rich milk
  or half 'n half
2 eggs plus 3 yolks;
  reserve egg whites for meringue

⅔ c. sugar
½ tsp. cinnamon
dash each of nutmeg and salt

In a mixing bowl combine all ingredients and beat together well. Spoon the cooled applesauce into the pie crust. Smooth with a large flat spoon. Over this pour the egg custard. Put in the oven at 350° and bake until the custard is well set and pastry is browned, about 40 minutes.

Meringue

3 egg whites   ½ c. sugar

Beat the remaining egg whites with ½ cup of sugar until stiff enough to form peaks. Pile onto the pie and return it to the oven. Bake just until the meringue is a pale buff color. Cool before serving.

TULE GREEK GRAPE PIE

The wild grapes gathered by Indians and settlers alike filled many pastries such as this.

1 9" pie crust plus another
  cut into lattice strips
3 c. seeded ripe grapes
1 T. flour
1 c. sugar
  or powdered ginger
½ tsp. grated fresh
  or powdered ginger
2 T. cider vinegar or
  the juice of a lemon plus
  some of the grated peel
1 egg white, slightly beaten

Line a pie pan with pastry. Combine grapes, flour, sugar, ginger, and vinegar in a bowl and stir. Fill the lined pie pan with the grapes and top with a lattice of pastry strips. Paint the crust with slightly beaten egg white and sprinkle with sugar.

GRAPE PIE

Margaret Daniel's western ancestors returned to the East, but she still makes their grape pie, a treat on either side of the Mississippi. She lives in Williamsville, New York.

2 rich pastry crusts
1 qt. grapes, stems removed
3 T. flour
1 scant c. sugar
1 T. butter

Slip skins from grapes; set skins aside and place pulp in saucepan. Cook pulp until soft, then press through sieve. Add to skin and mix. Combine flour and sugar and blend; then combine with grape mixture. Stir well. Line 9 inch pie plate with pastry. Add grape filling and dot with butter. Moisten edges. Cover with decorated top crust. Bake at 425° 20 minutes, and at 375° 25 minutes.

GOOSEBERRY PIE

The early settlers loved gooseberry pie; the later settlers loved gooseberry pie. You'll love gooseberry pie, too, topped with a tempting chunk of cream cheese.

2 9-inch pie crusts
4 c. gooseberries, hulled
4 T. flour or 2⅔ T. tapioca
  2 T. cornstarch
  dissolved in ¼ c. water
¾ c. sugar or more
½ tsp. cinnamon, ginger or
  nutmeg (or combine
  spices to taste)
1½ T. butter

Thicken the gooseberries with flour, tapioca or cornstarch. Add sugar. Let the mixture stand for 15 minutes. Mix in spices. Add more sugar to taste.

Spoon the fruit into the pie shell and dot with butter. Cover with a top crust or lattice and bake at 450° for 10 minutes. Reduce heat and bake 40 - 45 minutes.

GOOSEBERRY TARTS

1 recipe pie crust
1 qt. gooseberries
1½ c. water
1½ c. sugar

Form pie crust into tart shells and set aside. Stew gooseberries, water, and sugar together for 10 minutes. Fill shells with berry mixture and bake at 350° 15-20 minutes or until tarts are just browned.

PLUM DUMPLINGS

Dumplings were favorites on the frontier. When you bake these sweet dumplings, you can stick in your thumb, pull out a plum, and say "What a good cook I am."

Plum Sauce

8 plums, halved and pitted
1 c. sugar
¾ c. water
1 lemon, grated rind of lemon
dumpling batter
cream for topping

In a saucepan with lid place plums, sugar, water, and lemon. Bring to a boil. Spoon dumpling over sauce. Cover and boil gently for 25 minutes. Serve at once.

Dumpling Batter

½ c. plus 2 T. flour
¾ tsp. baking powder
2½ tsp. sugar
1/8 tsp. cloves
¼ tsp. cinnamon
¼ c. butter

Sift dry ingredients into a bowl. Cut in butter. Add milk, mixing lightly. Do not beat.

Plum Dumplings

BLACKBERRY DUMPLINGS

2 qt. blackberries	2 T. shortening, melted
2 c. water	1 tsp. baking powder
1 c. sugar	flour

In a large saucepan bring berries and 1 cup of water to a boil over medium heat. Add the sugar and stir well. Mix remaining cup of water, the shortening and the baking powder with enough flour to make a stiff dough. Roll out thin on a floured board and cut into small pieces. Bring the sweetened berries to a rolling boil and drop in the pieces of dough one at a time. Cook over high heat about 5 minutes and then simmer about 10 to 12 minutes more with the cover on. Remove from heat and let stand about 5-10 minutes before removing lid.

SUNDAY SPECIAL Alias BLACKBERRY DUMPLINGS

The Western pioneers had a limited supply from the mercantile store; yet they were content to make the best of what they had. Billy Jack Tabor of Sierra Vista, Arizona, invites us to "live off the land" with this wholesome dessert. These old West desserts were respectable and nutritious. This recipe uses a dropped dough as opposed to a rolled dough in the previous recipe.

1 c. sifted flour	3 T. shortening
1¼ tsp. baking powder	½ c. milk
¼ tsp. salt	1 quart ripe blackberries
1 c. plus 2 T. sugar	¼ c. water

Sift the flour, baking powder, salt and 2 tablespoons of sugar together. Cut in shortening with a pastry blender to make coarse crumbs. Add the milk and mix to make a soft dough. Combine the berries, 1 cup sugar, and the water. Bring to a boil. Drop the dough by tablespoons into the boiling fruit. Simmer uncovered for 10 minutes. Cover and cook 10 minutes more. Serve with cream or ice cream.

SOUTHERN MOLASSES PIE

This Southern pie went west with the immigrants. Molasses was a popular ingredient with southerners and westerners alike.

1 plain pastry shell	2 eggs
1 c. molasses	¼ tsp. salt
½ tsp. butter	

Line 9" pie pan with pastry shell and set aside.

Boil molasses and butter a few minutes. Break eggs into a bowl; add salt, and beat until well mixed. Pour molasses over eggs and stir very briskly. Pour into the pastry shell and bake at 350° for 15 minutes and 325° for 30 minutes more. Top with meringue if desired.

BEEHIVE APPLE PIE

Mormons must have a sweet tooth, maybe to compensate for their lack of consumption of alcohol, coffee and tea. The handcart-pushing Mormons made this on the trail and after they founded the Beehive state.

pastry for a 2-crust pie, unbaked	2 T. quick tapioca
6 large cooking apples, or the equivalent in crisply cooked ones prepared from dried fruit	½ c. honey
	½ tsp. each of ground cinnamon and nutmeg
	2 T. butter

Line a 9-inch pie pan with pastry. Peel and core the apples, if fresh, and cut into thin slices. Mix the apples with tapioca, honey, and spices. Spoon the mixture into a pastry-lined pan. Dot the top with butter. Cover with a second round of pastry; moisten the edges with water and seal. Cut a few slits in the top. Bake in preheated oven (375°) 40 to 45 minutes, or until the crust is done to your liking. Makes six to eight servings. Best when cooled slightly and served warm.

SOUR APPLE PIE

Pioneers loved apple pie so much that they sometimes served it as their main course. Sour apples make the best apple pie. Here is a recipe from Edith Schiller of Laurel, Montana.

pastry for double crust pie	6 c. tart apples, enough slices (peeled or unpeeled) to fill your pan
½ c. honey or ¾ c. sugar	
¾ tsp. cinnamon	
¼ tsp. nutmeg	1 T. water
¼ tsp. ginger	

Line pie pan with pastry. Mix the sweetening and spices. Add to apples and mix well. Heap in lined pan. Add the water. Adjust top crust and cut slits for steam to escape. Seal edges and flute. Bake in a hot oven (400°) for 50 minutes, or until crust is well browned and apples are cooked through. If necessary to keep edge from excessive browning, cover with strip of foil.

APPLE PIE WITHOUT THE APPLES

Without apples folks still make apple pie. Their recipe for pie filled with crackers is still popular today. Julie Anton, of Palo Alto, California, took this version from Ellen McGown Biddle's memoirs, *Reminiscences of a Soldier's Wife*, filling in the scanty instructions. Mrs. Biddle assures her gentle readers, "You will feel sure that it is apple pie."

5 c. unsalted soda crackers	½-1 tsp. nutmeg
⅔ c. warm water	1 pie tin lined with pastry and pastry for top
1 T. lemon juice	
1 c. sugar	

Break crackers into bite-size pieces; soak in warm water until soft. Sprinkle with lemon juice. Combine sugar and nutmeg; mix with cracker mixture. Put the mixture into the pie tin. Add a top crust, cutting slits or puncturing with fork. Bake at 400° for 30-45 minutes.

SELF-CRUSTING DUTCH OVEN APPLE MIT STREUSEL

When apples were available and the wagons stopped long enough, westerning pioneers baked this pie. If you don't want to cook with coals, you can bake this in your electric or gas oven at 350° or even a covered electric skillet.

6 c. tart apples, sliced
1¼ tsp. cinnamon
¼ tsp. each nutmeg, ginger and cloves
1 c. sugar or honey
¾ c. milk

½ c. self-rising flour, or all-purpose flour with
½ tsp. mixed baking powder and soda
2 eggs
2 heaping T. lard or butter

Have a good fire going. Grease a 10-inch Dutch oven. Mix apples with spices. Turn into Dutch oven. Beat remaining ingredients together with heavy spoon until smooth as possible. Pour over apples. Sprinkle with streusel (below). Set oven on bed of coals, not red. Heat lid in fire until hot. Place lid on oven and cover with coals. Bake about 45-50 minutes. Lift lid and test for doneness. Serve this pie hot or cold. Top with cream for a special dessert.

Streusel

Mix 1 cup self-rising flour, ½ cup chopped nuts, ½ cup brown sugar, and 3 tablespoons lard or butter. Mixing ingredients, work until crumbly.

FRUIT FRITTERS

1 c. flour
1 tsp. baking powder
½ tsp. salt
¼ tsp. nutmeg
2 eggs

½ c. water
assorted fruits of your choice cut in bite-size pieces

Sift dry ingredients. Beat eggs and combine with water. Blend both mixtures together. Dip prepared fruit in fritter batter. Deep fry in melted fat at 375° for 2-3 minutes. Drain.

STRAWBERRY PIE

At Hattie Nevin's cafe in Coquelle, Oregon, strawberry pie was the specialty. Its fame spread far and wide.

2 c. boiling water
½ c. sugar
1 small box of strawberry gelatin powder or a package of unflavored gelatin
1 T. lemon juice

2 c. sliced strawberries, plus more for topping pie
1 pie crust
½ pt. whipping cream

Into the boiling water add the sugar, gelatin, and lemon juice. Let stand until partially set. Put this in the pie shell with the strawberries. Let stand until cold. Add the whipped cream, spreading decoratively on top of the pie. Add more berries on top, with a whole berry in the center. For a less sweet pie, cut the sugar.

CUSTARD PIE WITHOUT EGGS OR MILK

Besides apple pie without apples there was custard without eggs or milk. These privation recipes offer Old West proof that necessity is the mother of invention. Julie Anton adapted this custard recipe from one recorded in *Let Them Speak For Themselves: Women in the American West, 1849-1900.*

6 T. cornstarch
2 c. cold water
1 T. lemon juice
¼ c. sugar

Combine cornstarch, water, lemon juice, and sugar. Fill six 5-ounce custard cups (or heat-proof little dishes) with mixture. Set in shallow pan on oven rack. Pour 1 inch hot water into pan. Bake at 350° for 40 minutes. Serve in custard cups or bake the custard in a pie shell.

SILVER PIE

A most unusual "coconut flavored" pie, made from potato, is silver pie. The original recipe came from *An American Cookbook,* written by an American orphan and printed for Elijah Brooke in 1812; one copy of that rare volume is owned by Edith J. Schiller of Laurel, Montana.

1 pie paste or pastry crust recipe

Pie Filling

1 large white potato,
  peeled and grated
1 lemon, grated and juiced
4 egg whites
1 c. sugar
1 c. cold water
1 T. lemon or anise flavoring
jam or jelly

Combine potato, lemon juice and rind, the beaten white of 1 egg, ¾ cup sugar, and 1 cup water. Beat well.

Bake in a pie paste at 425° for 10 minutes and at 350° to 375° for 20 minutes more.

After baking, spread pie with the beaten whites of 3 eggs well frothed and sweetened with ¼ cup sugar. Flavor with lemon or anise and return to the heat to brown.

Lay on small bits of jam or jelly when served, perhaps 8 T. crabapple.

GRAPEFRUIT COBBLER

Living in California, the family of Winnie Thorne, of Santa Rosa, always had access to grapefruit. They used them to best advantage in this mouth-watering cobbler.

1 recipe regular pie dough
3 large or 4 small grapefruit
½ c. or more sugar
lots of butter

Peel and section the grapefruit, removing all of the white skin. Lightly mash the sections in a bowl; add sugar to taste. Put a layer of grapefruit in your favorite baking pan. Roll out half of the pie dough very thin and cut into inch wide strips. Lay strips over fruit in pan, trimming to fit pan. Spoon in remaining fruit with lots of butter. Roll out remaining dough, cut into strips and lay over fruit at right angles to first layer of dough strips. You will have a layer of grapefruit, a layer of pie dough strips running one direction, another layer of grapefruit, and another layer of dough strips running in the other direction. Sprinkle with sugar and butter. Bake at 350° until the top is nice and brown, about 50 minutes.

DRIED FRIED FRUIT PIES

Davilla Bright says that you can fry these pies in a greased skillet or in a pot of hot fat.

1 double recipe for pie paste
2 c. water
3 c. dried fruit, apples or peaches
½ c. sugar, or to suit your taste
lard or fat for frying
cheese and/or syrup for topping

Simmer the apples or peaches in a saucepan with water until tender but not mushy, 20-30 minutes. Add sugar to taste.

Prepare crust while dried fruit cooks. Roll pieces of pie dough into half circles, about five inches in diameter. Spoon about 4 T. of the fruit onto one end of each dough piece. Fold dough over fruit, making a quarter circle. Brush the edges of the dough with sugar water before sealing to prevent filling leakage. Fry in a well greased skillet, until crust is brown. Turn so that both sides are cooked. Or deep fry in hot fat.

Serve hot or cold with slices of cheese and syrup topping.

Fruit, Stewed and Poached

STEWED APPLES AND RICE

Apples weren't just for pies. They teamed up deliciously with rice. Peel and core baking apples. Put the apples in a deep baking dish. Pour over them a syrup made by boiling 1 pound of sugar added to a pint of water. If the apple syrup is too thin, boil it to thicken. Put a little piece of shredded lemon inside each apple and let them bake slowly until done but not in the least broken. Put a little jam inside each apple and little heaps of boiled rice between them. Serve hot or cold.

POACHED STRAWBERRIES IN HONEY

Simmer berries in warm honey no longer than ten minutes.

Cakes

MOLASSES CAKE

There were no boxed mixes in 1870, and a cook's recipes did not always have ample instructions. Instead, stored knowledge was called for when baking these recipes for molasses cake and sponge cake. Katharine Place of Tucson, Arizona found the recipe cards with her aunt's belongings a long time ago.

½ c. sweet milk
1 tsp. dry yeast
½ c. butter
½ c. sugar
1 egg, beaten
½ c. molasses
2 c. flour
1 tsp. cloves
1 tsp. cinnamon

Warm milk and add yeast. Let bubble. Cream butter and sugar and add beaten egg. Add molasses, sifted flour, and spices to the yeast mixture. Pour mixture into 8-inch round cake pan. Let rest in warm place for half an hour. Bake in oven at 350° for about 45 minutes.

ANGEL FOOD CAKE

Women used to be judged as bakers on the quality of their angel food. Air, beaten into the whites of eggs, is the only leavening agent. The tube pan is the baking utensil found most successful.

1 c. sifted cake flour
1½ c. sugar
1½ c. egg whites
¼ tsp. salt

1½ tsp. cream of tartar
1½ tsp. vanilla extract
½ tsp. almond extract

Sift the flour and ¾ c. of sugar together several times. Beat the egg whites with salt and cream of tartar in a large bowl at high speed of the mixer—or by hand with a whisk—until light and fluffy. Sprinkle the remaining sugar over the egg whites, 2 tablespoons at a time, beating thoroughly after each addition. Continue beating until stiff peaks form. Fold in extracts. Sift the dry ingredients, 2 tablespoons at a time, over the beaten egg whites. Fold in gently but thoroughly with a wire whip or rubber spatula. Pour the batter into an ungreased tube pan. Make sure that there is not a trace of any fat in the pan. Cut gently through the batter to remove large air bubbles. Bake in a preheated moderate oven (350°) for 40 to 50 minutes, or until the crust is golden brown and the cracks are very dry. Invert the pan immediately and place on a funnel or bottle. Cool the cake in the upside-down pan for at least 1 hour. Cut the cake out of the pan with a sharp knife. Slice the cake with a serrated knife using a sawing motion or use two forks to separate the cake into pieces. Yields 10 to 12 servings.

SPONGE CAKE

6 eggs
2 c. sugar

1½ c. water
3 c. flour

Beat eggs and gradually add sugar; then add water and sifted flour, simultaneously. Pour mixture into 2 greased 8" to 9" round or square cake pans or a tube pan. Bake at 350° for 30 minutes.

PORK CAKE

When the family bought some citron and candied fruit at the store they made pork cake like the one Jean Peterson contributed. Jean's recipe for imitation coffee is in Chapter 1.

1 lb. fresh pork fat
1 pt. boiling coffee
 to pour over the fat
1 lb. raisins
¼ lb. citron, nuts,
 or any candied fruit,
 store bought or homemade
2 c. sugar
1 c. molasses

1 tsp. soda, dissolved in molasses
1 oz. nutmeg
1 oz. ginger
2 oz. cloves
2 oz. cinnamon
flour

Combine all the ingredients except the flour. Add enough flour to make the consistency of a regular cake batter. Bake at 350° until done, about 45 minutes.

Ingredients for Scripture Cake

SCRIPTURE CAKE

The pioneer housewife or ranch wife didn't always get to church. In her spare time, though, she could make a cake by consulting her Bible. Walt Thayer's version is similar to a pound cake. Another version resembles a fruitcake.

1 c. Judges 5:25 (last clause)
2 c. Jeremiah 6:20
2 tsp. Samuel 14:25 (last clause)
6 Jeremiah 17:11
1 c. Judges 4:19 (last clause)
4½ c. I Kings 4:22 (proportion to taste)
2 heaping tsp. Amos 4:5
1 c. I Samuel 30:12 (2nd phrase) to taste

Combine all the ingredients and pour into a greased 10-inch Bundt pan or 2 7-inch loaf pans. Bake at 375° for 30 minutes and your cake should be done.

DRIED APPLE STACK CAKE

Stack cake was a traditional wedding cake made or at least put together at the wedding celebration. Each guest brought a layer of cake. Applesauce made from fresh or dried apples was spread on each layer. The bride's popularity could be measured by the number of stacks she had and by the number of layers in each stack. This same idea of stack cake was sometimes used at other get-togethers. Although the layers were often of various colors and flavors, this recipe is for a simple molasses cake, typical of pioneer times. Mrs. Carl Teasley, of Ocoee, Tennessee, submitted this Colorado version, which doesn't call for eggs. The dough makes good soft cookies, too. There are no complete directions for this old-time cake; just use kitchen know-how.

- 1 c. butter
- 1 c. brown sugar
- 1 c. sour milk
- 7 c. sifted all-purpose flour or part whole wheat flour
- 1-1½ c. molasses
- 1½ tsp. soda

Make a soft dough; it should be thin and make 5 layers. Knead the dough like a biscuit. Press the dough into pans with hands. The pans should be greased, round 8½-inch cake pans. Bake at 350° for about 25 minutes. If you don't have enough pans, bake in shifts.

To make applesauce, cook the apples; sweeten and spice with ginger and cinnamon to taste. Mash the apples and beat them to a sauce Spread between the cake layers. Canned applesauce will do in a pinch.

GRANDMA'S GINGERBREAD

Mrs. Alice Jacobs of Ekalaka, Montana, still relies on her grandmother's formula for good gingerbread.

In a large crock or bowl put:

lump of lard and beef tallow mixed, the size of a big egg—about ½ c.
2 handfuls of sugar—about 1 c.
2 eggs, beaten
2 glugs of black syrup molasses—a glug is when you pour out of a gallon jug of molasses and it says "glug." 2 glugs equals about ½ c.
½ gill of sour milk—a gill is a c. or ¼ pt.-¼ c. milk
3 handfuls of flour—about 1½ c.
one 2-finger pinch of salt and allspice—about ¼ tsp.
one 3-finger pinch of soda—about ½ tsp.
one 4-finger pinch of baking powder—about 1 tsp.
one 3-finger pinch and one 4-finger pinch of ginger—about 1½ tsp.

Beat all together and bake in a greased 7 x 10-inch pan at 350° until a broom straw inserted in the middle of the cake comes out clean, about a half-hour.

BARE CUPBOARD CAKE

When the cupboard was bare, the frontier woman was forced to invent new dishes. She substituted and improvised to turn nearly nothing into something special. Take, for example, vinegar pie, cake without eggs or milk, pea sausage, and mock oysters—they are all substitutes for other dishes.

1 c. sugar
½ c. shortening
½ tsp. salt
1½ c. water
½ c. raisins
1 tsp. cinnamon
1 tsp. cloves
1½ tsp. nutmeg
1 tsp. baking soda, dissolved in
  a T. of warm water
2 c. flour

In a small pan, boil the sugar, shortening, salt, water, raisins, cinnamon, cloves, and nutmeg for 5 minutes.

Let the ingredients stand until cool. Add the baking soda and the flour. Bake in a cake pan for 30 minutes at 375°.

ROSE GERANIUM CAKE

During the Civil War, rose geranium leaves were commonly used as a flavoring. The cake named for the plant was especially popular.

12 rose geranium leaves
1 c. butter, divided into 6 pieces
1 ¾ c. sugar
6 egg whites
3 c. cake flour, sifted
4 tsp. baking powder
½ tsp. salt
¾ c. milk
½ c. water
favorite recipe for plain frosting
  flavored with rose extract
  instead of vanilla

Rinse leaves. Wrap six leaves around each stick of butter. Wrap and chill overnight. Remove leaves from butter; rinse and set aside. Cream butter and sugar until light. Add egg whites, two at a time, beating well after each addition. Sift together flour, baking powder and salt. Mix milk and water. Alternately add flour mixture and liquid to butter mixture, beating smooth after each addition. Grease and flour two 1½-inch deep and 8-inches in diameter round pans. Arrange six leaves in each pan; spoon batter evenly into pans. Bake at 350° for 30 minutes. Remove from pans and cool on racks. Gently remove leaves from cakes and discard. Fill and frost with rose frosting.

CARROT CATTAIL CAKE

The cattail was an invaluable food source. For the Indians and pioneers of the West. Bill Newton of Alabama cautioned cattail gatherers to be wary of snapping turtles!

To gather cattail pollen: Put mature cattails in a bag or sack and shake. The spikes should release their golden pollen. Cattail pollen makes good biscuits and pancakes. It is perfect for rolling fish in for frying. It is a cause for wonderment as to whether the Indians made carrot cake, but Carolyn Niethammer, authority on Southwest cooking, submitted this recipe.

½ c. cattail pollen
1 c. flour
1 c. sugar
1 tsp. baking powder
1 tsp. salt
1 tsp. cinnamon
½ tsp. soda
⅔ c. salad oil
2 eggs
1 c. grated carrots
½ c. crushed pineapple
1 tsp. vanilla

Sift together dry ingredients. Add oil, eggs, carrot, pineapple and vanilla and beat. Spread in a greased 8 or 9-inch square pan and bake at 350° for 35-40 minutes.

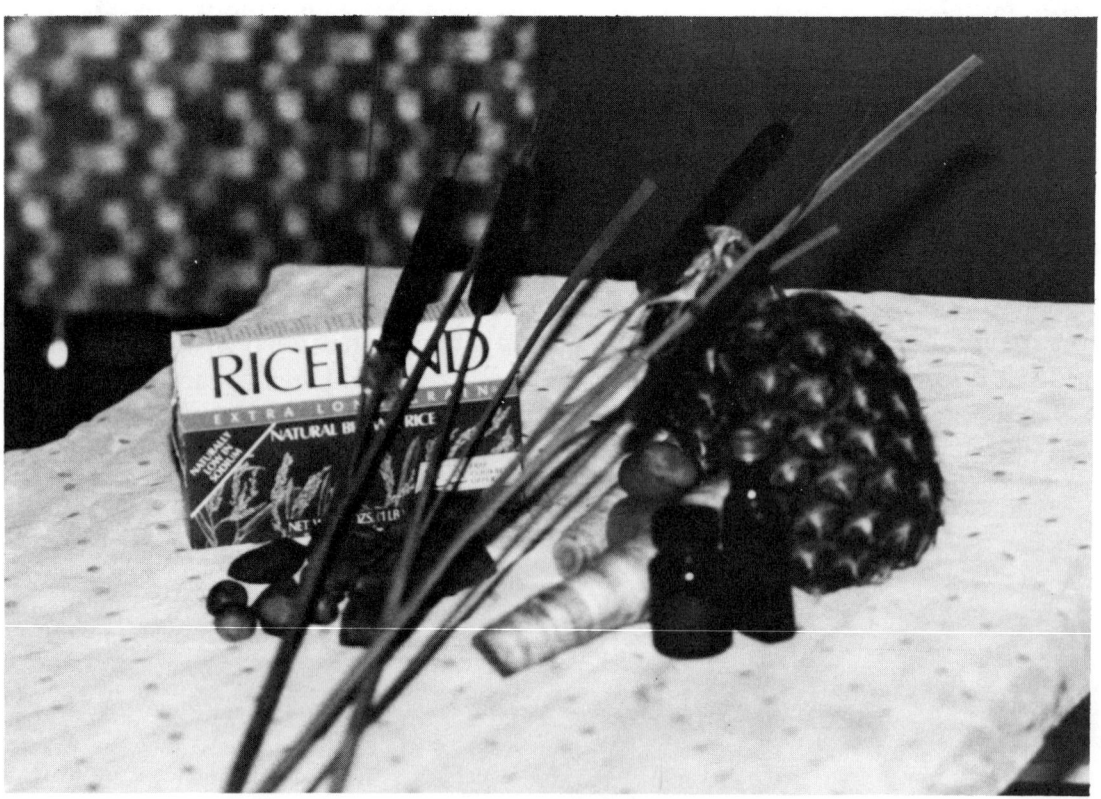

Ingredients for a Carrot Cattail Cake

STRAWBERRY SHOW-OFF DESSERT

This seems pretty elegant for the Old West, but Don Getz's family made it in Nevada, many years ago.

2-3 oz. packages strawberry gelatin
½ tsp. salt
2½ c. boiling water
2 c. fresh or frozen strawberries
1 pt. heavy cream
1 small angel food cake or sponge cake
(pg. 118 of this chapter)

Dissolve gelatin and salt in boiling water. Allow to chill until partially set. Whip, then fold in the strawberries and whipped cream.

Break cake into bite-size pieces. Place half of broken cake pieces into bottom of greased cake pan. (A bundt cake tin does nicely.) Pour half of strawberry mixture over cake pieces. Add remaining cake pieces and then top with remaining gelatin mixture. Chill until set, preferably overnight. Decorate with whole strawberries and serve.

CHRISTMAS PUDDING

A traditional pudding resembles a cake. This one takes about 30 days in a dark place to ripen and mellow.

¼ lb. seedless raisins
½ lb. unseeded raisins
½ lb. candied citron, lemon and orange
½ lb. figs, chopped
4 c. bread crumbs
½ lb. beef suet, chopped
½ c. flour
1 tsp. cinnamon
dash salt
½ tsp. cloves
½ c. brown sugar
6 eggs, beaten
½ c. cider or fruit juice
sherry flavoring

Mix the fruits, crumbs and suet. Then add the flour, spices, salt and sugar. Next, add the eggs and cider or juice and sherry flavoring. Place dough in a buttered 3-qt. pudding mold or 2 buttered 1½ qt. molds. Cover tightly with a double thickness of wax paper or aluminum foil; secure with string. Place on rack in bottom of large kettle and add boiling water to half cover mold. Cover and steam for 3 hours. Unmold. Serve warm or let it ripen and mellow. Dip the cloth in brandy to cover the pudding as it mellows. If you want to serve it flaming, warm a liquor such as brandy or rum. After it has been ignited, pour the flaming alcohol over the pudding. If it is served for Christmas, decorate it with a sprig of holly.

PRUNE KUCHEN

A prune cake from the German immigrants is as good as pie. Don Getz took this recipe from the old family cookbook.

1 c. all-purpose flour
2 T. sugar, granulated
  cane or beet
¼ tsp. salt
½ c. butter, softened

Combine flour, sugar, salt, and butter. Mix with pastry blender until the butter is evenly distributed.

Put the pastry in a greased 8-inch square pan. Pat evenly over bottom and up the sides to make crust. Bake at 425° for 15 minutes.

Filling

2 c. pitted prunes, about 40
½ c. granulated sugar
½ tsp. cinnamon
2 egg yolks
1 c. sour cream

Combine filling ingredients and spoon into crust. Bake at 325° 20-30 minutes.

RYE RINGS

This cookie was a natural for the ladies on the frontier because it was made with rye flour. The dough can be cut into stars instead of rounds and sprinkled with cinnamon sugar.

1 c. butter
½ c. sugar
1 c. rye flour
1½ c. sifted all-purpose flour,
  more or less

Cream the butter and gradually add the sugar. Stir in the rye flour first. Mix thoroughly, then add the other flour. Chill the dough for 30 minutes. Work with a little of the dough at a time. Knead the dough slightly and roll it out as thin as possible between two sheets of waxed paper. Prick the surface with a fork all over. Cut out rounds with a cookie cutter; cut the center from the cookies with a thimble, or cut rounds with a doughnut cutter. Place the cookies on a buttered and floured cookie sheet, using a spatula. Bake in a preheated moderate oven (350°) for 8 to 10 minutes, or until golden. Cool on cookie sheets. Yields about 30 three-inch cookies.

BLACK WALNUT WAFERS

2 eggs
1 c. light brown sugar
⅔ c. all-purpose flour, sifted
¼ tsp. salt
1 tsp. baking powder
1 c. finely chopped black walnuts

Beat eggs until light. Add sugar and beat until thick. Add sifted dry ingredients and nuts; mix well. Drop by scant teaspoonfuls onto greased cookie sheets. Bake in preheated 400° oven for 5 minutes. Let stand for ½ minute before removing from sheet. Makes about 5 dozen.

MESQUITE GINGER COOKIES

The controversial mesquite tree is a veritable food factory, according to many cooks, Carolyn Niethammer among them.

2-inch piece fresh ginger root
1 c. shortening
1 egg
¾ c. honey

1 c. whole wheat flour
1 c. mesquite meal
2 tsp. baking powder
¼ tsp. salt

Peel ginger root and grate. Beat shortening and egg together until smooth and fluffy. Add honey and ginger and beat until combined. Add flour, mesquite meal, baking powder and salt. Beat well.

Drop by teaspoonfuls on greased cookie sheet. Dampen the corner of a clean tea towel and wrap it around the bottom of a juice glass. Flatten each dab of cookie dough with towel-covered glass.

Bake in preheated oven at 325° about 12 minutes or until lightly browned. Makes about 4 dozen.

MEDAL COOKIES

Use two colors of jam to make these cookies look like ornaments. To give a quaint old-fashioned flavor to the frosting use rose water. Before the vanilla vogue, rose water was common.

¾ c. butter
⅓ c. sugar
1 egg
2 c. sifted all-purpose flour

¼ tsp. salt
jam and/or jelly
confectioners' sugar
frosting

Cream the butter. Gradually beat in the sugar and egg. Add the flour and salt. Blend well. Chill 30 minutes. Roll the dough out thin and cut into two-inch rounds. Put on greased cookie sheets and bake in a preheated oven (350°) for 10 minutes or until lightly browned. Cool. Put two cookies together with jam filling and ice with the frosting. Center a dab of jelly on the top of each cookie. Yields about 15 two-inch double cookies.

Frosting: Put 2 tablespoons of hot water in a small bowl. Add a dash of salt and ¼ tsp. of vanilla extract or ½ tsp. of rose water. Gradually beat in 1½ cups of confectioners' sugar, or enough to make a frosting of spreading consistency.

ANTLER COOKIES

½ c. butter
½ c. sugar
2 egg yolks
1 egg, beaten
2 tsp. ground cardamon

¼ c. heavy cream or
  evaporated milk
2 c. sifted all-purpose flour
1 c. cornstarch
1 tsp. baking soda

Cream the butter and beat in the sugar. Beat in the egg yolks, egg, and cardamom. Beat in the cream. Sift together the flour, cornstarch, and baking soda. Add to the batter and mix thoroughly. On a lightly floured board, roll the dough to ¼-inch thickness. Cut the dough into 1 x 2 inch pieces. In each piece, about ¾ inch from each end, make a crosswise cut not quite the width of the dough. Pull both ends to make a curve, so that the cuts open a little. Bake on greased cookie sheets in a 350° oven for about 15 minutes, until golden brown. Yields about 3 dozen.

ALMOND COOKIES

Scandinavia is not the only place to find Christmas platters heaped with Mandelterter, Ragkakor, Medaljekager, and Hirvensavret. Since the 1840s when the Norwegians settled in the old West, followed in the '50s and '60s by the Swedes, Danes, Finns, and Icelanders, Christmas cookery west of the Mississippi has felt the influence of Scandinavia.

½ c. butter
½ c. sugar
1 egg yolk, beaten
½ c. finely chopped almonds
1½ c. sifted all-purpose flour

Cream the butter and beat in the sugar. Add the egg, almonds, and flour. Mix well and chill. Use a cookie press or roll the dough on a lightly floured board and cut into S shapes or crescents.

Bake on lightly greased and floured cookie sheets in a preheated moderate oven (325°) for 8 to 10 minutes. Let cool. Store the cookies between layers of waxed paper in a covered tin or jar. Yields 4 dozen or more cookies.

ALMOND TARTS

The dough for almond cookies can also be used to make tarts. Fit it into tart or muffin pans to bake. After baking, fill the shells with cream or fruit fillings.

Scandinavian Christmas Cookies and Homemade Cordial

SPICY MOUNTAIN ROCKS

Don Getz has saved his grandmother's recipe for cookies. The original recipe, circa 1885, called for raisins with heavy seeds and pinenuts. Try them with either pinenuts or walnuts.

1 c. water	1 tsp. baking powder
2 c. raisins, pitted or seedless	1 tsp. baking soda
1 c. lard or shortening	1½ tsp. allspice
2 c. granulated sugar	½ tsp. nutmeg
2 eggs	½ tsp. cinnamon
4 rounded c. flour	1 c. walnuts

Put water and raisins into a quart saucepan. Boil for about 3 minutes; then set aside to cool.

In a large mixing bowl, cream shortening and sugar until fluffy. Add eggs and beat until thoroughly combined. Add cooled raisins to mixture.

Add flour, baking powder, baking soda, allspice, nutmeg, cinnamon, and nuts; beat well to blend.

Drop by teaspoonfuls onto a well-greased baking sheet. Bake at 350° 12-15 minutes or until done. If eaten while warm, they are chewy and delicious. But if they're left uncovered or lightly covered for several hours, a hammer can hardly crack them. Dunk them in hot coffee or cold milk, to make them chewy again.

INDIAN ICE CREAM (Whipped Berry Dessert)

This is a simple dessert. You can vary the amount of berries and the sweetening to your taste. Originally, the Indians probably whipped some corn flour and fat with the fruit and syrup.

Mash 4 cups huckleberries or raspberries. Add honey, syrup, or sugar to taste, about 1 cup. Huckleberries need more honey than raspberries. Whip with beater or by hand. Chill before serving. You enjoy this even more if you top it with real whipped cream.

PULLED MOLASSES CANDY

Remember penny candy? If not made at home, this taffy could be purchased at the store. MaryAnne McDonald's family enjoyed the taffy pulls at home. As a little girl, though, MaryAnne once got a rope of it caught in her hair and had to have a lot of locks cut off. Beware—It's sticky!

3 T. butter	⅔ c. sugar
2 c. molasses	2 T. vinegar

Melt butter in kettle; add molasses and sugar, stirring until sugar is dissolved. Boil until hard but not brittle or until a little of mixture dropped into cold water forms a hard ball, stirring constantly at the last. Add vinegar, remove from fire and pour into greased pan. When cool enough to handle, butter your fingers and pull, but do not squeeze the candy. Pull until porous and light yellow. Cut in small pieces.

FRUIT LEATHER

This treat was taken to the one-room schoolhouse in an old lunch bucket.

Take uncooked dried fruits. Sprinkle them with lemon juice and force them through a food chopper with a fine blade. Add juice as needed. Spread the mixture on a sheet coated with wax paper. Form into rolls or strips.

PEPPERMINT "COUGH DROPS"

"Old recipes are such fun," says Edith Schiller of Montana. Here is one her grandmother sent to her mother when Edith was less than one year old and suffering from bronchitis.

½ c. sugar
2 T. water
5 drops peppermint or other flavor
a little color from a few drops of beet juice, optional

Stir sugar and water over low fire until sugar is melted; continue stirring for 5 minutes—no less—and add mint. Drop by ½ teaspoon on waxed paper and allow to cool.

NUT BRITTLE

2 c. granulated sugar
½ c. vinegar
½ c. water
butter, the size of a walnut
1 lb. assorted nuts and dried fruit of your choice

Place ingredients, except nuts, in an iron skillet; bring to a slow boil, stirring until thoroughly mixed. Boil until brittle or forms a hard ball (when dropped by spoonful) in cold water. Stir occasionally while cooking. This brittle has to be watched very carefully; when it is brittle it will be transparent.

Arrange peanuts or black walnuts, or other type nuts, figs, dates, and/or coconut on a buttered platter; pour the brittle over the nuts. It will cool quickly. When it cools break into pieces.

MINTED WALNUTS

Lisa Kendall, the mother of Katharine Place of Tucson, Arizona, made minted walnuts every year at Christmastime until she couldn't stir the mixture at the tender age of 92! She cracked each nut herself, placing it on a flat rock and striking it in just the right place. Then she would carefully extricate the unbroken halves.

1 c. sugar
½ c. water
1 T. white corn syrup
1 T. marshmallow cream
3 c. walnut halves
½ tsp. essence of peppermint

Put sugar, water, and syrup in saucepan. Boil for one minute. Add marshmallow cream; stir. Add nuts, and stir until walnuts are covered. Add peppermint and mix thoroughly. Put on waxed paper. When cool, gently break the pieces of nuts.

SQUAW CANDY

This recipe won't give you cavities.

To preserve salmon like the Northwest Indians, dry salted salmon that has been cut into strips. Eat this as a snack, like jerky.

HORSEY D'OEUVRES or COWBOY HORS D'OEUVRES

Yankees and city dudes both love this finger food, from Hollis W. Harris, of Amarillo, Texas. It can be served as an appetizer, a snack, or as a dessert.

- 2 T. butter
- 3 T. tomato sauce
- 2 T. brown sugar
- 1 T. apple cider vinegar
- 1 tsp. salt, optional
- ½ tsp. garlic powder
- ½ tsp. cinnamon
- 1 T. finely ground plain chili powder or 2 T. hot taco sauce
- 1 lb. fresh pecan halves

In a skillet melt butter; add tomato sauce, brown sugar, vinegar, salt, garlic powder, cinnamon, and chili. Add pecans and stir to coat thoroughly.

Bake at 300° in a single layer on baking sheet for 20-25 minutes or until brown and crisp. As an optional touch, you can sprinkle the finished product with pecan dust.

Spiced Nutmeats—cowboy style!

Chapter 10
HOUSEHOLD HINTS

Broken bits of licorice sprinkled about pantry shelves will, it is said, banish red **ants**.

Have in your kitchen a cheap office stool to sit on when ironing or washing dishes; this will prevent **backache** and tired feet.

A solution of soda and water applied with a whisk broom kept for the purpose will remove the brown streaks in **bathroom** bowls made by sediment in the dripping water; if the spots do not come off easily, let the solution stand a few minutes, and it will rub off very easily.

When cooking lima beans, rice, etc., it is very provoking when they foam and sputter onto a clean stove. Drop into the kettle a small lump of butter and there will be no **boiling over**.

A flannel wet with kerosene oil will remove fly speck from **brass**. Polish with chamois.

Bore a hole through the **broom handle** and slip a string through it so you can hang it up.

Cane-seated chair bottoms that have sagged may be made as tight as ever by washing them with hot water and leaving to dry in the open air.

Sprinkled salt on the **carpet** will collect the dirt quickly and prevent dust from flying all over everything.

Discolored **china baking dishes** can be made as clean as when new by rubbing them with whiting.

A pinch of borax in the cooked starch will make the **clothes** stiffer and whiter.

A woolen cloth dampened with gasoline will make the **dirt** disappear as if by magic.

Enameled **kitchenware** that has become burned or discolored may be cleaned by rubbing with salt wet with vinegar.

A currycomb makes an excellent fish scraper.

When using **fly paper**, it is apt to fall or come in contact with some article of furniture, floor, etc. After removing the paper, apply a generous amount of kerosene to the article of furniture or clothing and it will quickly remove the sticky substance. It does not injure clothing and readily evaporates. Try this and you will be pleased with results.

An equal mixture of turpentine and linseed oil will remove the white marks from **furniture** caused by water.

Salt water is preferable for cleaning bamboo **furniture**, as it prevents it from turning yellow, and is also good for wiping Chinese or Indian matting.

To clean the **frying pan** after frying, pour off the hot lard and wipe the pan with clean paper until all sediment is removed. It can then be easily washed.

To clean a **fishy frying pan** fill it with cold water and place on the fire to boil. When boiling, put a red hot ember in, then wash in usual way.

Equal parts of water and skimmed milk, warm, will remove fly-specks from varnished woodwork or **furniture**, and make it look fresh.

To wash a **glass** from which milk has been poured, plunge first into cold water before putting it into warm. The same rule holds good with egg cup or spoons from which eggs have been eaten.

A very important point in washing cut **glass** is to avoid sudden changes from extreme heat to extreme cold and vice-versa. A pitcher or tumbler which has been filled with ice water, a tray that has been used for ice cream, if plunged at once into hot water, will be apt to crack. Use tepid water and the risk of breakage is avoided.

Use a little ammonia in the dish water when washing **glassware**. It will make it sparkle like glass.

Salt, dissolved in alcohol, will often remove **grease** spots from clothing when nothing else will.

After broiling or frying, wipe off the fat that has spattered on the range with an old newspaper, thus keeping the top free from dirt and **grease**.

A little washing soda mixed in the blacklead will remove all **grease** and give grates and stoves an excellent **polish**.

If you spill **grease** upon a hot stove, cover the spot at once with a thick layer of ashes; this will absorb the grease, so you will not be offended by its odor while burning, and a little later you can brush away the ashes, and none of the grease will remain.

Save all the **grease** not suited for cooking and turn it into soap by the use of lye.

To remove **grease** from wood floors, sand is much better than soap for this purpose. If the floor is dirty mix a little chloride of lime with the sand. You will need plenty of warm water.

In the emergency of illness, when no refrigerator is at hand and **ice** is not regularly kept, a block of ice may be best kept by placing it in a stone crock of sufficient size after wrapping the ice in wet newspapers; the jar should then be thoroughly surrounded with a feather pillow; it will keep in this manner several days.

To retard the melting of ice in the **icebox**, cover the top of it with wet paper.

By placing a rubber fruit ring under a dish that is being placed on ice, the ring will stick to both ice and dish, thus preventing it from slipping.

For stings or bites from any kind of **insect**, apply dampened salt. Bound tightly over the spot it will relieve, and usually cure very quickly.

If one insists on using **kerosene** as a fire kindler, better pour a pint or so into an old tin pail and stand as many corncobs or pieces of board or kindling in it as the pail will hold overnight. The cobs will be thoroughly saturated by morning and are not so dangerous to use.

Loose **knife handles** are easily mended. Take the handle off, mix together three parts resin and one of brick dust. Nearly fill the handle with this, heat the steel beyond the blade till nearly red hot, insert in the handle, and press down into place. It will be firm as when new.

A few stalks of rhubarb cut up and boiled in a teakettle full of water will soften the deposit of **lime** so that it may be all scraped away.

Vinegar removes **lime** spots.

The **lime** deposit which forms in the bottom of a teakettle can be removed by boiling vinegar in the kettle.

Marks from perfume may be removed from the tops of bureaus and dressers by rubbing with a cloth dipped in kerosene or oil and turpentine.

The **mica windows** of coal stoves can easily be cleaned with a soft cloth dipped in vinegar and water. This should be done when putting the stove up.

The **mixing pan** can be quickly cleaned if a little boiling water is poured into it for a few minutes and a close cover put over. The steam softens the dried dough so that it will readily wash off.

After removing all dust, wipe screen doors with kerosene, and they will look new and as long as the odor remains **mosquitoes** and moth millers will give them a wide berth.

A panful of lime kept in the cupboard with your jams and preserves will prevent **molding**.

To stop **mouse holes**, stuff with plugs of common hard soap, and you will do it effectually. Rats, roaches, and ants will disregard it.

The lid of a teapot should always be left so that the air may get in. This prevents **mustiness**. The same rule, of course, applies to a coffee pot.

The **odor** that clings so persistently to a utensil in which fish or onions have been fried may be dispelled by placing in hot oven for ten or fifteen minutes after washing and drying.

To remove the **odor** of onions from a knife dip it into cold water, then dry and polish it. Hot water tends to set the odor of onions both on the knife and the hands, and for this reason should be avoided.

Sour milk added to the water with which **oilcloth** or linoleum is washed, gives it a luster like new. In fact, any kind of milk is good.

A double layer of brown paper on the pantry shelf and kitchen table covered with **oilcloth** will enable the oilcloth to last longer.

When an **oven** is too hot for the proper baking of what is in it, put a basin of cold water inside. As the water becomes hot add more cold water and in this way keep the oven at the desired temperature.

To take anything hot from the **oven** have a stiff wire with a hook at the end.

Do not put **pans** and kettles partly filled with water on the stove to soak, as it only makes them more difficult to clean. Fill them with cold water and soak away from the heat.

Boil a little vinegar in frying **pans** before washing them.

Clean the keys of the **piano** with a soft cloth dampened with alcohol, wipe quickly with a clean, dry cloth.

Waste **pipes** may be cleaned of soap and slime by placing a handful of common salt in the bottom of the basin overnight. The salt will gradually melt and the first flush of water in the morning will clear the pipe.

By mixing enough flour of sulphur with a pint of water to give a golden tinge, and in this boiling three bruised onions, you can renovate your gilt **picture** frames.

Rub the **range** with a soft cloth moistened with a few drops of deodorized kerosene; this should keep it clean.

Rats and mice can be driven away by putting potash into holes or where they are likely to go.

Clean the **rollers** of the clothes wringer with gasoline and be careful to wipe off all superfluous oil from the cogs and crank that the clothes may not be soiled by the oil that has been on the cogs.

Lemon juice and salt will remove iron **rust**.

Kerosene will remove the gummy substance which forms on new **sewing machines**.

It is said that if a small piece of camphor be placed in a silver chest the **silver** will not become discolored.

Hot sour milk will brighten **silverware**.

A soap that will get you clean is made from lye. Here's the recipe:

LYE SOAP

Dissolve 1 can of lye in 2½ pints of hot water. Let cool. Then pour lye solution in a slow easy stream into the melted fat, stirring constantly. Continue stirring until cool. Pour into boxes that have been dipped in cold water. Cut in desired size of squares when cold and set. Bobbye Herzberg of Elsberry, Missouri, contributed this recipe that was the March, 1984 Recipe of the Month.

Small scraps of **soap** tied into a cloth or bag are excellent for cleaning bathtubs, graniteware, etc.

When a tea or coffee pot has become **stained** inside, fill with cold water, add a teaspoon of soda. If set upon the stove and boiled for three-quarters of an hour, the inside will become as bright and clean as new.

To prevent **tea kettle crust**, put a large marble inside the kettle.

Baking **tins** are easily kept smooth if scoured with Bon Ami and then washed after they have been used.

Tinware may quickly be cleaned by rubbing it with a damp cloth, dipped in soda.

To prevent **wooden bowls** from cracking immerse them in cold water; then set over the fire, bring to the boiling point and let boil an hour, and don't take them out until the water has gradually cooled.

Hang this above your automatic washer; when you think you have too much work and read it.

GRANDMA'S "RECEET" FOR WASHING CLOTHES

Years ago a grandmother gave a new bride the following "receet" for washing clothes. It appears below just as it was written and despite the spelling has a bit of philosophy. (Submitted by Mrs. Alice Jacobs of Ekalaka, Montana.)

1. Bilt fire in back yard to heat kittle of rain water.
2. Set tubs so smoke won't blow in eyes if wind is pert.
3. Shave one hole cake of lie soap in bilin' water.
4. Sort things. Make three piles. 1 pile white. 1 pile cullord. 1 pile work britches and rags.
5. Stir flour in cold water to smooth. Then thin down with bilin' water
6. Rub dirty spots on board. Scrub hard. Then bile. Rub cullord, don't bile, just rench in starch.
7. Take white things out of kittle with broom stick handle. Then rench, blew and starch.
8. Spread the towels on grass.
9. Hang ol' rags on fence.
10. Pour rench water on flour beds.
11. Scrub porch with hot, soapy water.

12. Turn tubs upsode down.
13. Go put on clean dress, smoth hair with side combs, brew cup of tea, set and rest and rock a spell, and count blessings.

With those non-edible recipes the reader is at first reminded that success is the result of perseverance and application. If you fail, try again.

CULINARY CUES

Before Heloise there were aids to help the cooks solve cookery problems.

Almonds are blanched by scalding them with boiling water.

If the top of a **cake** is sprinkled with flour as soon as it is turned from the pan the icing will spread more easily and will not be so likely to run. Before the cake is iced most of the flour should be wiped off.

To keep a **cake** fresh for several weeks, take it from the oven, and while still hot, pack it completely in brown sugar.

Heavy **cakes** are often the result of using damp fruit. After washing, currants and raisins should be left in a colander in a slightly warm place for twenty-four hours.

To freshen shredded **coconut**, soak it in sweet milk a few minutes before using it.

A pinch of soda stirred into milk that is to be boiled will keep it from **curdling**.

A tiny pinch of salt added to **coffee** before the boiling water is poured on will accentuate the flavor.

To keep **cookies** from burning on the bottom turn the baking pan upside down and bake on the bottom of the pan.

Put a handful or two of tissue paper torn into shreds in the bottom of the **cookie jar**. This allows the air to pass through, keeping the cookies good and crisp.

To improve the flavor of boiled **corned beef**, add a small onion, a few cloves, a pinch of ginger, and a bay leaf.

When **cream** will not whip add the white of an egg, both being chilled to same temperature; it will then whip easily.

In a **custard** recipe calling for several eggs, some of the eggs may be left out by substituting for each egg omitted one-half teaspoon cornstarch.

A tablespoon of vinegar in the lard in which you fry **doughnuts** will prevent them from being greasy.

When cracked **eggs** have to be boiled, some vinegar added to the water will prevent the white from boiling out. The vinegar coagulates the albumen and stops the leaks.

To cut hard-boiled **eggs** in smooth slices, dip the knife in water.

A pinch of salt will make the white of an **egg** beat more quickly.

When **fruit ferments**, reheat it, add a little sugar and make it up into pies or tarts.

Open canned **fruit** an hour or two before it is needed for use. It is far richer when the oxygen is thus restored to it.

Ginger **cookies** mixed with cold coffee instead of milk have a delicious taste.

To keep **icing** soft, add a pinch of baking soda to the white of the egg before beating them, then beat and proceed in the usual way.

To keep **lemons** fresh a long time invert over them a glass or earthenware dish that fits closely.

Grate the rinds of four lemons in half pint of alcohol. Shake frequently and at the end of four weeks you will have a fine **lemon extract**.

Dry **lettuce** by blotting with soft paper, patting it carefully to prevent bruising.

Save all **liquids** from mustard or spiced pickles and use them in salad dressings or for mixing with meat for sandwiches.

Save the **liquor** from pickled peaches, etc. because it may be used in places where wine was formerly used, such as mince pies, etc.

In cooking tough **meat** or fowl, one tablespoon of vinegar in the water will save nearly two hours boiling.

A platter of cold **meat** is nicely garnished with slices of lemon.

When filling gems or **muffin pans**, leave one of the small sections empty and fill it half with water—the gems will then never scorch.

Mixed **mustard** will keep its color if a pinch of salt be added.

Do not use **newspapers** to wrap about anything edible.

A little boiling water added to an **omelette** as it thickens will prevent it from being tough.

An **oven door** should never be slammed when anything is baking.

To bake **potatoes** quickly, boil them in salted water for ten minutes, then put in the oven. The boiling water will heat them through so they cook in a short time.

Before baking **potatoes**, peel them and rub them with butter or bacon. The outside, when baked, will be a delicate brown, which can be eaten with the rest of the potato.

In order to have **potatoes** always white, the kettle in which they are cooked should never be used for any other purpose.

Hot milk added to **potatoes** when mashing them will keep them from being soggy or heavy.

If roasted **potatoes** are burst with a fork they will be found much lighter and more digestable than if cut with a knife.

Pumpkins should be kept in a dry part of the cellar, apples in a moderately dry part; turnips should be kept in a damp part of the cellar.

When making a steamed or boiled **pudding**, put a pleat in the cloth at the top to allow for the pudding to swell.

For all **salads** containing fruits or fish, lemon juice is much nicer than vinegar, when available.

After boiling **salt beef**, leave two or three carrots in the liquid until cool; these absorb the salt and the liquor may be turned into soup.

To prevent milk from **scorching** when scalding, rinse the pan in water to moisten it before putting in the milk.

Instead of wasting **skimmed milk**, make it into cottage cheese.

If **soup** is too salty, add slices of raw potatoes and boil a few minutes until saltiness is reduced to taste. The potatoes may then be used in many ways.

Stale bread may be refreshed by slicing and wrapping first in a dry cloth, then in a moist towel around it and the whole placed in a covered jar or icebox.

Restore **stale crackers** by placing them in a warm oven for a few minutes.

If vinegar is added to prunes and similar dried fruit when **stewing**—about 3 tablespoons to a pound—it will improve the flavor.

In making fruit pies, the **sugar** should not be put on top, but between two layers of the fruit because sugar next to the top crust toughens it.

Sugar in fried cakes, fritters, etc. should always be added to the milk; this prevents the cakes from absorbing the fat in the frying.

A little baking soda added to boiling **syrup** will prevent it from crystalizing; a little vinegar likewise will prevent syrup from returning to sugar.

To keep **vegetables** fresh and cool, place them in a deep pan or dish with cold water to half cover them; over them spread a folded wet napkin, allowing the corners to dip into the water; place on window or other place where cool air can reach them.

In cooking **vegetables**, cover those that grow under the ground, as turnips, onions, etc.; leave uncovered those that grow above the ground.

A slice of lemon in a glass of **iced tea** will make it "Russian Tea."

If a small pinch of salt is added to every gallon of water boiled for drinking purposes, it will not have that flat, insipid taste common to boiled water.

To **warm over** biscuits, rolls, muffins, etc. sprinkle lightly with water, place them in a pan and set this pan in another containing a little hot water; place in oven until just right.

For a **whipped lemon filling** for a cake, put half a pound of sugar in a bowl, add grated and juice of one lemon and half a cup of boiling water. Whip stiff and spread between cake layers.

One generous teaspoonful of vinegar added to the water in which **whitefish** are boiling will be found to improve the flavor very decidedly. It also has a tendency to make the flesh firm without toughening it.

HERE'S TO HEALTH AND BEAUTY

Old time doctors prescribed crushed eggshell for babies, a wheat grain amount per bottle, and proportionately greater amounts as they grew older.

Keep your baby occupied by putting molasses on his fingers, and give him a feather to play with. It'll keep him occupied for hours.

For **blackheads**, wash several times a day with a good soap. Rinse well with clear water. Dry with a coarse towel, massaging as you dry. Avoid rich foods and get lots of exercise.

To stop **bleeding**, bind a cloth soaked in lemon juice to the cut or wound.

Also, try old cobwebs compressed into a lump and applied to the wound.

To restore the color to black kid **boots**, take a small quantity of good black India ink, mix it with the white of an egg, and apply to the boots with a soft sponge.

As a remedy for a **burn**, apply sweet oil, scrape the inside of a raw potato, lay in place, securing with a rag. Replace potato often, if burn is severe, better send for the doctor.

For **chapped hands**, boiled potatoes are said to cleanse the hands as well as common soap; they prevent chaps in the winter season and keep the skin soft and healthy.

For **chilblains** or frosted feet, dip feet every night and morning in cold water for a minute or two, and dry by rubbing very hard with a coarse towel. Or put them immediately into brine brought from a pickle tub.

To greatly relieve a **cold**, try a hot lemonade.

To make a **cold medicine**, boil cut up onions with honey in water to cover.

Simmer until onions are soft. Then strain and bottle. This recipe is from my mother Dorothy Breeding of St. Petersburg, Florida.

To make **cologne water** take one gallon of alcohol and add the following: twelve drams oil of lavender, four drams oil of rosemary, twelve drams oil of bergamot, twelve drams essence of lemon, and twelve drops oil of cinnamon.

To soften **corns**, apply cloth soaked in lemon for several nights. The corns can then be pared off.

To make a **corn poultice**, mix Indian meal and cold water till the mixture is a mush consistency. Wrap the poultice around the toe. In two to three hours remove the poultice and the corn will be soft enough to cut some off with a knife or scissors. Repeat until corn is entirely leveled. There is no way to get rid of the corn completely.

If your **feet blister** from walking to town, cover the soles of your stockings with brown, homemade soap.

To cure **dandruff**, to one quart of water, add one ounce of sulphur. Shake well every two hours, and saturate the head every morning with the liquid.

Gargle with a strong solution of lemon juice and water for a bad sore throat.

To cut the oil on **hair** that is too greasy, add a few drops of lemon juice to the shampoo.

To prevent and cure a sick **headache**, take a strong lemonade before breakfast.

To cure a sick **headache**, take one teaspoonful of pulverized charcoal and one-third teaspoonful of soda mixed with water. You don't have to buy Bufferin.

To stave off **hunger**, there's nothing like chewing coffee grounds.

To soften hands roughened by labor or cold, apply Indian meal and vinegar. The mixture will heal them.

Wash fruit-stained **hands** with lemon juice.

For **mosquito** bites, also bee stings or bites from any venomous animal, mix salt into a paste with vinegar and plaster it onto the bite.

For people for whom **perspiration** is a problem, take a bath with some ammonia in the water. Alum borax added to the bathwater is also effective. Powder parts most affected with talc or rice powder.

To cure a **pimpled face**, and sweeten the blood, put one ounce of Sena in a small pot and pour a quart or more of boiling water on it; then put as many prunes as you can get in. Cover it with paper and set in the oven with household bread. Take this every day or when needed.

For a **rash**, apply the juice of the aloe vera leaf.

When **recuperating** from an illness, drink eggnog and eat "graveyard stew," milk toast, buttered and covered with hot milk.

When in need of a **restorative**, try a raw egg mixed with sugar and a little wine. Beat this until frothy.

To bring about relief and reduce the swelling from **rheumatism**, add lemon juice to milk until it curds. Then bind this upon the parts swollen.

For **ringworms**, apply mercurial ointment at bedtime.

Sheep nanny tea was a frontier remedy for sickness. When pioneers came west on the old Oregon Trail their only medicine for sickness was those remedies given to them by other pioneers. You gathered some sheep droppings or pellets that were dry and firm, with no dirt on them; then you put them in a pot and added boiling water. After you strained the "tea" through cheese cloth and added some ginger and sugar it was ready to drink. After drinking a cup of this potent "tea'" anyone with a bad case of Epizootic or Gadsa Hoolah (parasites) would be back to normal in 24 hours. It wasn't as well known as "Buffalo Chip," but did the job when there were sheep pellets available to make the Sheep Nanny Tea. Just ask Walt Thayer.

To treat **warts**, touch carefully with a new pen dipped in aquax-fortis. Repeat.

RECIPE FOR MAKING A FASHIONABLE WOMAN—from **Idaho World 4-25-1872**—submitted by Walt Thayer

Take 90 pounds (or more) of flesh and bones—mostly bones, wash, cleanse and bore holes in the ears; bend the neck to conform with the Grecian bend, the kangaroo droop, the Saratoga slope or bullfrog beak, as the taste inclines. Then add 3 yards of linen; 100 yards of ruffles and 75 yards of edging; 18 yards of dimity; one pair silk-cotton hose with patent hip attachments; one pair of false calves; 6 yards of flannel, embroidered; one pair Balmoral boots with heels 3 inches high; 4 pounds whalebone in strips; 1,760 yards of steel wire; ¾ of a mile of tape; 10 pounds of raw cotton or two bushel; 4 copies of *The World*; 150 yards of silk or other dress goods; 500 yards of lace; 1,400 yards of fringe and other trimmings; 12 gross of buttons; one box of pearl face powder; one saucer of carmine and an old hare's foot; one bushel of false hair frizzed and fretted a la manique; one bundle of Japanese witches with rats, mice and other varmints; one peck of hairpins; one lace handkerchief, nine inches square, with patent holder. Perfume with attar of roses or "Blessed Baby" or "West End." Stuff the head with fashionable vowels, ball tickets, playbills, wedding cards, some scandal, a lot of wasted time and a very little sage. Add a half-grain of common sense, three scruples of religion and modicum of modesty. Season with vanity, affection, and folly. Garnish with earrings, finger rings, breast pins, chains, bracelets, feathers and flowers to suit the taste. Pearls and diamonds may be added . . . Whirl all around in a fashionable circle and stew by gaslight for six hours. This dish is highly ornamental, a "piece de resistance" for the head of your table upon grand occasions but, being somewhat indigestable and highly expensive, is not reccomended for daily consumption in the home.

LAUGHTER—THE BEST MEDICINE—THE BEST RECIPE

An Idaho senator always left his door unlocked so that hungry travelers could go in and cook themselves a meal. Never was anything stolen except his sourdough, in which he took special pride; so he bought a new "slop jar" and put his sourdough in it and set the jar under his bed. It was never stolen again.

--

The pie social was second to the dance in popularity with women doing their best to make better pies than their neighbors. On one occasion in an Idaho town, Grandma Blake received the honor. After listening to an evening of praise of her ability, and particularly of the fine job she did in crimping the pie crust, she announced she did the crimping with her new set of store teeth.

--

Carnation milk even advertised in stock newspapers that it would give a prize for the best jingle written praising the product. One ranch wife eagerly sat down and wrote:

> Carnation milk, best in the lan',
> Comes to the table in a little red can.

She gave it to the cowboy to mail, then waited with excitement to hear from the company. She heard. By letter they told her they could not use her poem because it was unfit to print.

The wife was at first angered, then bewildered, then confused. She called the cowhand and demanded an explanation. Had he altered her letter?

The cowboy grinned a shy, slow grin, then reddened under her boiling gaze. "Well Ma'm," he said, "I read your poem an' figured it was too short. I wanted to see you win that prize, so I figgered I could add a verse and make it better."

"Then what in creation did you write?"

"Oh I jes' give it a little more punch by making it read:

> Carnation milk, best in the lan',
> Comes to the table in a little red can.
> No teats to pull, no hay to pinch,
> Jes' punch a hole in the sonobitch."

(This was contributed by M. Butchee of La Mesa, Texas.)

An important ingredient in an Old West cookbook is the famous poem about dried apple pies. The author is unknown—perhaps Apple Crocker.

DRIED APPLE PIES

I loathe, abhor, detest, despise,
Abominate dried-apple pies.

I like good bread; I like good meat,
Or anything that's fit to eat;

But of all poor grub beneath the skies,
The poorest is dried apple pies.

The farmer takes his gnarliest fruit;
Tis wormy, bitter, hard, to boot;

He leave the hulls to make us cough,
And don't take half the peeling off.

Then on a dirty cord 'tis strung
and in a garret window hung;

There it serves as roost for flies,
Until it's made up into pies.

Tread on my corns, or tell me lies,
But don't pass me dried apple pies.

What happened when sawdust was mixed with the chicken feed? One of the hens hatched out ten little woodpeckers. Walt Thayer swears by Paul Bunyan that this really happened to him in the early days of Idaho during the spring following a very cold winter. The old hens had a "woody" flavor for stew. And the pin feathers served as toothpicks.

From those days when a cowboy first rode across Texas soil he developed a strong, almost vehement dislike for milk and cream, especially in his coffee. He didn't mind herding cattle, but he'd be damned if he would drink their milk. He didn't mind his breath smelling of whiskey and tobacco but he certainly didn't want it to smell like that of a young calf.

In time, canned milk made it to the plains. Women were delighted. Cowmen did not even like to talk about it. Charlie Russell once pulled a can of Eagle Brand from a cook's shelf and said, "I think it came from that bird. It's a cinch it never flowed from an animal with horns."

Besides ringing the dinner bell, meals were announced by more than the usual "Come and get it." Davilla Bright remembers her father saying "Get your feet under the table." And her neighbor used to say "You can sit up now."

The perfect ending for a perfect book is the perfect ending for a perfect day as found in a poem by an unknown author, often referred to after a day of activities such as feeding the pigs and helping to get them back into the pen. To get her life back in order Great-grandma could identify with this poem.

GRANDMA'S TRANQUILIZER

Grandma, almost any day,
Did a washing, mopped the floors,
Cleaned the windows, did some chores;
Swept the parlor, made the bed;
Baked a dozen loaves of bread;
Split some firewood, lugged it in,
Enough to fill the kitchen bin;
Churned the butter, baked a cake,
Then explained, "For Goodness Sakes!
The pigs have gotten out the pen,"
And went and chased them in again.
She gathered eggs and closed the stable;
Went back in and set the table;
Cooked a supper quite delicious,
And afterward washed all the dishes;
Fed the cat and sprinkled clothes;
Mended a basketful of hose;
Then opened the organ and began to play,
"When You Come to the End of A Perfect Day"

Index

BEVERAGES

Bee Beer..................................8
Bishop...................................10
Campfire Coffee...........................5
Chocolate.................................5
Cowboy Coffee.............................3
Currant Wine..............................9
Elderberry Wine...........................9
Ginger Beer.............................6,7
Ginger Beer
   More Modest Version....................6
Gooseberry Wine...........................8
Hard Times Coffee.........................4
Herb Tea..................................5
Hot Spiced Applejack.....................10
Imitation Coffee..........................4
Milk Coffee...............................5
Molasses Beer.............................6
Mulled Cider.............................10
Mulled Wine..............................10
Quince Cordial............................9
Raspberry Cordial.........................9
Rose Cordial.............................10
Sangaree.................................10
Sassafras Beer............................7
Southwestern Mocha........................6
Spruce Beer...............................7

BATTERS AND DOUGHS

Acorn Bread..............................28
Alaska Sourdough Starter.................26
Arkansas Corn Bread......................18
Bannocks.................................15
Basic Ranch House Bread..................25
Bean 'N Onion Corn Bread.................20
Bishop Bread.............................27
Boiled Indian Bread......................16
Buckwheat Pancakes.......................14
Buttered Biscuit.........................25
Buttermilk Corn Bread....................21
Cheechako Bread..........................23
Chicken or Turkey Spoonbread.............19
Chuckwagon Sourdough Starter.............24
Cornmeal Batter Cakes....................17
Cornmeal Muffins.........................20
Corn Pone................................17
Cowboy Biscuits..........................27
Crackling Bread..........................19
Cracklin' Corn Bread.....................19
Cush.....................................16
Don's Flapjohns
   Sourdough Flapjacks...................13
Flannel Cakes............................13
Flour Tortillas..........................29
Green Corn Griddle Cakes.................15
Griddle Cakes............................14
Grit Bread...............................16
Homemade Yeast...........................24
Huckdummy................................28
Icebox Sourdough Biscuits................26

Meat Pie with Corn Bread Topping.........22
Mexican Corn Bread.......................21
Mission Loaves...........................22
Navajo Fry Bread.........................30
Oatmeal Bread............................23
Oatmeal Muffins..........................28
Orange Cracklin' Bread...................17
Pioneer Hominy...........................16
Potato Yeast.............................25
Quick Loaf Bread.........................28
Railroad Yeast...........................24
Rye 'N Injun.............................20
Salt-Rising Bread........................22
Sausage Scrapple.........................18
Scrapple.................................18
Skillet Corn Bread.......................17
Sopaipillas..............................30
Sourdough Biscuits.......................26
Sweet Dumplings..........................15
Whole Wheat Waffles......................14

PUDDINGS AND PORRIDGES

Baked Indian Pudding.....................36
Champurrado..............................34
Fruited Indian Pudding...................36
Graham Porridge..........................33
Grandma's Gruel..........................37
Hasty Pudding............................32
Indian Meal Pudding......................35
Lumpy Dick...............................32
Mission Corn Pudding.....................34
Pease Porridge...........................34
Pima Pumpkin Pudding.....................35
Poor Man's Soup..........................37
Son-of-a-gun-in-a-sack...................33
Spotted Pup..............................36
Wagon Trail Corn.........................36

SOUPS AND STEWS

Apache Corn Stew.........................41
Apache Corn Stew
   According to Euell Gibbons............41
Basic Chili..............................48
Bean Hole Beans..........................51
Beef, Beans and Beer.....................42
Beef Gumbo...............................43
Cheese and Potato Soup...................40
Chili Verde
   (or Speedy Gonzales Chili)............50
Chili With Beans.........................49
Chuck Wagon Stew and Dumplings...........44
Dumplings.............................50, 51
Dutch Oven Stew..........................46
El Puchero
   (Meat and Vegetable Stew).............47
Escalloped Turkey Casserole..............52
Fish Stew................................53
Grandma's Bean Soup......................40
Hobo Stew or Jungle Stew.................46
Hungarian Pepper Stew....................52
Indian Meal Pudding......................35

Old West Cookbook — 143

Loggers' Stew 46
Menudo 53
Mulligan Stew 47
New Mexico Chili Con Carne 49
Onion and Nasturtium Soup 41
Poet's Son-of-a-Bitch-Stew 45
Piggie Stew with Corn Dumplings ... 50
Ribs and Dumplings 51
Simple Sorrel Soup 39
Son-of-a-Bitch Stew 45
Tash Pashota 40
Victory Soup 42
Webster's Chowder 43

MEAT, POULTRY, FISH

Baked Hash 63
Blackbird Pie 69
Braised Bear 57
Buffalo Bear 57
Buffalo Jerky 55
Buffalo Roast 55
Buffalo Stew 56
Buffalo Tongue 56
Calf's Head 70
Chicken Pie 67
Cornish Pastries 68
Fried Meat Cake or
  Pioneer Hamburger 63
Fried Trout 60
Frizzled Beef, I and II 62
Green Peppers with Buffalo 57
Holiday Goose 65
Indian Salmon 61
Klook (Blood Meat Balls) 70
Mammy's Stuffed Squatum Crabs 66
Mona Basin Stuffed Trout 61
Mountain Dip Steak of Lean 64
Onion Stuffing (For Goose) 65
Pemmican 57
Poached Trout or Salmon 60
Reed Birds 58
Roast Venison 58
Roasted Wild Turkey With
  Herbed Corn Bread Stuffing 59
Rocky Mountain Oysters 70
Sauerkraut Stuffing 66
Sausage in Savory Gravy 64
Sole A La Marguery
  A La Diamond Jim Brady 69
Spicy Chocolate Stuffing 63
Suckling Pig 67
Sunday Chicken Pies 68
Texas Style Swiss Steak 58
Trout with Mint 61
Veal Loaf 64
Wild Turkey 59

VEGETABLES

California Picnic Salad with Dressing 78
Cattail Bud Pilaf 74
Cole Slaw 80
Condiments
  Almond Flavoring 82
  Catsup 82
  Chili Gravy 81
  Curry Powder 81
  Flavored Vinegar 82
  Lemon Extract 82
  Mustard 82
  Perky Porky Barbecue Sauce 83
  Southwest Chili Sauce 81

Corn on the Cob 75
Cowboy Salad 79
Creamed Corn 75
Dandelion Fritters
  (Cornmeal Hush Puppies) 73
Food and Friends 83
Fried Huckleberries or Blueberries 75
Fried Turnips 79
Granny Special 73
Green Beans with Bacon 78
Green Beans with Onion 80
Green Corn Oysters 78
Green Tomato Gravy 79
Ham and Bean Bake 79
Hominy Grapple 77
Indian Mushrooms 75
Meat Stretcher 76
Mexico Pinto Beans 79
Oklahoma Slaw 80
Onion Pie 77
Parched Corn 76
Pea Sausage 78
Pokesalad 73
Popcorn for Dinner 76
Preserving Root Vegetables 83
Sauerkraut 81
Skillet Potatoes with Onions 78
Smothered Potatoes 78
Squash Fritters 79
Sweet 'n Sour Lettuce 80
Wagon Trail Corn 76
Wild Greens 74
Wild Onions 73
Wild Rice with Mushrooms
  and Hickory Nuts 75

EGG AND DAIRY PRODUCTS

Baked Alaska 90
Bee Balm Pudding 89
Bird's Nest Pudding 88
California Zephyr French Toast ... 85
Fillin' 87
Ginger-Peachy Ice Cream 89
Hangtown Fry 87
Hopi Omelette 86
Make-Believe Lemon Pie 89
Old Time Butter Making 88
Piperade 86
Pueblo Hominy and Eggs 87
Smierkase—Cottage Cheese 88
Tansy Omelette 86

RELISH AND PRESERVES

Bell Pepper Relish 96
Canning Cues 92
Chokecherry and Gooseberry Relish 95
Fancy Mincemeat 100
Ham 99
Honey Without Bees 95
Imitation Maple Syrup 92
Large Green Peppers Stuffed
  with Pickled Cabbage 97
Lemon Balm Jelly 94
Methodist Mince Meat 101
Mince Pies 101
Mom's Chow Chow 96
Mulberry Jelly 95
Piccalilli 95
Pickled Beets 98
Pickled Cauliflower 99
Pickled Eggs, Modern Recipe 98

Pickled Eggs, Old Fashioned Recipe.....98
Pickled Fish..........................99
Pieplant Preserves....................94
Plum Bread Pudding....................94
Plum Jelly............................94
Plum Preserves........................94
Sauerkraut............................96
Savory Goose Spread..................101
Tomato Preserves......................96
Western Soup.........................102
Wild Plum Jam.........................93

DESSERTS

Air Pie..............................108
Almond Cookies.......................125
Almond Tarts.........................125
Angel Food Cake......................117
Antler Cookies.......................124
Apple Pie Without the Apples.........113
Applesauce Custard Pie...............109
Bare Cupboard Cake...................120
Beehive Apple Pie....................113
Blackberry Dumplings.................112
Black Walnut Wafers..................123
Blueberry Cream Pie..................108
Carrot Cattail Cake..................121
Christmas Pudding....................122
Custard Pie Without Eggs or Milk.....114
Dried Apple Stack Cake...............119
Dried Fried Fruit Pies...............116
Fresh Raspberry Pie..................109
Fruit Fritters.......................115
Fruit Leather........................127
Gooseberry Pie.......................110
Gooseberry Tarts.....................110
Grandma's Gingerbread................119
Grapefruit Cobbler...................114
Grape Pie............................110
Horsey D'oeuvres
  or Cowboy Hors D'oeuvres...........128
Indian Ice Cream
  (Whipped Berry Dessert)............126
Medal Cookies........................124
Mesquite Ginger Cookies..............124
Minted Walnuts.......................127
Molasses Cake........................116
Nut Brittle..........................127
Nut Custard Pie......................106
Osgood Pie...........................107
Peppermint Cough Drops...............127
Pies.................................104
Plain Pastry Shell, I................104
Plain Pastry Shell, II...............105
Plain Pastry Shell, III..............105
Plum Dumplings.......................111
Poached Strawberries in Honey........116
Pork Cake............................117
Prune Kuchen.........................123
Pulled Molasses Candy................126
Raisin Vinegar Pie...................107
Rich Pastry Shell....................105
Rose Geranium Cake...................120
Rye Rings............................123
Scripture Cake.......................118
Self-Crusting Dutch Oven
  Apple Pie Mit Streusel.............115
Silver Pie...........................114
Sour Apple Pie.......................113
Southern Molasses Pie................112
Spicy Mountain Rocks.................126
Sponge Cake..........................117

Squaw Candy..........................128
Stewed Apples and Rice...............116
Strawberry Pie.......................115
Strawberry Show-Off Dessert..........122
Sunday Special
Alias Blackberry Dumplings...........112
To Roll Out a Pie Crust..............105
Tule Greek Grape Pie.................110
Vinegar Pie..........................107

Culinary Cues........................133
Dried Apple Pies.....................138
Grandma's 'Receet' for Washing Clothes 132
Grandma's Tranquilizer...............139
Health and Beauty....................135
Household Hints......................129
Laughter—Best Medicine...............137
Lye Soap.............................132
Recipe for Making A Fashionable Woman 137
Useful Table for Housewives..........140
Weights and Volumes..................140

Old West Cookbook — 145